Listening Skills Training

How to Truly Listen, Understand, and Validate
for Better and Deeper Connections

from various sources. Please consult a licensed professional before attempting any techniques outlined in this book.

By reading this document, the reader agrees that under no circumstances is the author responsible for any losses, direct or indirect, which are incurred as a result of the use of information contained within this document, including, but not limited to, — errors, omissions, or inaccuracies.

Table Of Contents

Table Of Contents

Your Free Gift

As a way of saying thanks for your purchase, I'm offering the book ***Bulletproof Confidence Checklist*** for FREE to my readers.

To get instant access just go to:

https://theartofmastery.com/confidence/

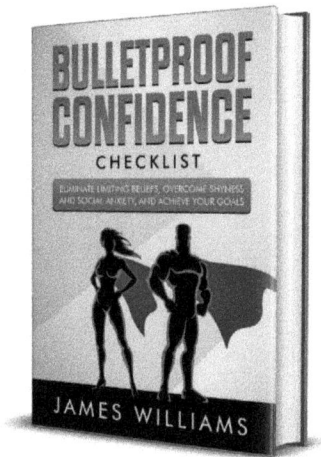

Inside the book, you will discover:

- Why we develop shyness & social anxiety
- Powerful strategies for overcoming social anxiety
- Become more confident by destroying these negative traits

- How to easily prevent the "awkward silence" in a conversation
- Confidence checklist to ensure you're on the right path of self-development

Introduction

"Listening is an art that requires attention over talent, spirit over ego, others over self." Dean Jackson

Are you listening?

More and more, I, like many others all over the world, am coming to a very real and somewhat saddening realization. I apologize in advance if it's something you haven't noticed before, but now that I say it, you're never going to be able to unsee it.

There are so few people out there who are good listeners. In fact, I'd go as far as to say most people are actually terrible.

Just last night, I sat down after work and started to watch the news. There was some debate being aired about LGBT movements, which is, of course, an important topic of conversation that needs to be spoken about. Except, despite being live and on-air to potentially hundreds of thousands of people, every person at the desk was shouting over one another. These so-called experts and professional broadcasters, the supposed top of their fields, were shouting over one another, not allowing anyone to be acknowledged, heard, or understood.

There was no conversation or discourse taking place here. Just shouting, ego-boosting, and playing "gotcha!" with one another. Honestly, it was pretty disgraceful and made me fairly sad that this is where we have gotten to as a society, especially with important issues like that.

I turned the television off and sat in the silence of my apartment, a thought started to form in my mind. Poor listening is everywhere. Literally everywhere. It's an epidemic.

It occurs in politics, on reality television shows, across the internet in comment sections across every platform. Few people are listening at work, in the street, and, most importantly, in your own personal relationships.

After a bit of research, it turns out that even when it comes to communicating and understanding the people we love the most, many of us fail to listen properly and actually hear the person talking to us. The chances are you've felt this yourself. You've experienced your partner listening to you firsthand, and although they are listening to the words you're saying, they do not actually hear you and your message. On the flip side, the chances are you've been the individual who's not been listening to others. I know without a doubt I'm guilty of being that guy.

Looking back with hindsight, it feels as though I've been living my life on autopilot, especially when it comes to my relationships with partners. I couldn't seem to keep a relationship for more than a year for much of my early life. They almost always seemed to conclude with a dramatic and explosive end. I told myself I hadn't perhaps met the one yet and that when I did, everything was going to come together perfectly, and I'd find my happily-ever-after. Of course, that was never going to happen. Still, it wasn't until years later that I can look back and say with a strange cocktail of confidence and embarrassment that the problem was me and, predominantly, my lack of ability to listen.

I'll share an example, and you can see whether you can figure out for yourself what the problem is. I'll set the scene. I'm sitting at the table in my apartment. My girlfriend gets in from work and sits down at the table like we do every night. I've cooked dinner, we start eating, and after a bit of small talk, my girlfriend, who we'll call Nicole for this example, says this:

Nicole: "Work is just so stressful. I think I'm going to start looking for another job because I seriously have no idea how much longer I can take this," she said, swirling her glass in her hand.

Me: "Do you think you'll find one that pays as well, though?"

Nicole: "I don't know."

Me: "What kind of job would you like to do if you could do any?"

Nicole: "I don't know."

Me: "Well, I wouldn't give up the one you have until you find something else to replace it."

It makes my body feel tense whenever I replay that conversation in my head, especially with the knowledge and skills I have now. It's one of those memories that burn vividly in the back of my mind.

Besides the point, did you see what went wrong in that conversation?

Quite clearly, I wasn't listening to my partner properly, if at all.

For brevity, I'm going to jump straight to the point. There's no reason to dress this up because being able to listen to someone is one of the most important skills you'll ever learn. You know when you Google *How to have a better relationship,* or you watch a movie featuring a scene with couples counselling, and they always talk about how the best thing a relationship can do to be better is get better at communicating? Surprise, they're not wrong. I just wish I'd known it earlier.

Mastering the art of listening brings so many benefits to your life and the lives of those around you.

In the conversation with my partner, you can clearly tell that I'm not listening because I'm injecting my own thoughts into the conversation, piggybacking what my partner is talking about and making the conversation all about me than taking the opportunity to connect with her. I'm failing to dive any deeper into how she is feeling or thinking. This is the girl I was supposed to love, and I didn't even let her explain how she felt.

Now imagine how often this happens to you. And how many times do you do that to other people? As I said before, poor listening is truly an epidemic.

Here's a rewrite of how the conversation should have gone had I been a skilled listener.

Nicole: "Work is just so stressful. I think I'm going to start looking for another job because I seriously have no idea how much longer I can take this."

Me: "Hey. Talk to me about it. What's going on?"

Nicole: "Where do I start? The managers treat me awfully. My coworkers are horrible. The work is tedious and unrewarding. The hours suck. I never get to spend time with you anymore. God, listen to me

7

moaning. I should be grateful to even have a job in the current climate."

    Me: "No, it's okay. Anyone would feel like that in your situation. Do you think you're holding onto the job because you feel you should be grateful for it?"

    Nicole: "I guess that's part of it."

    Me: "Well, is there anything you do like about your current job?"

And so on. Can you see how much of a difference there is in both conversations?

I'm not forcing my narrative or my own ideas into the conversation, hijacking the talk with the forced desire to communicate my own needs. Instead, I'm stepping up and allowing Nicole to express herself, to go into detail about how she feels, asking questions so I can gain much more clarity and understanding about how she feels, and, most importantly, I'm enabling her through validating her experience.

Validation. The absolute key to any successful conversation or interaction. In the first version of the conversation, you'll fail to find any sign of validation, and I'm sure you've felt this way in your own life. Those moments where you've opened up to someone, and they respond in such a way that it feels as though they took nothing of what you said on board and are instead pursuing their own agendas, using the opportunity to share how they feel, rather than listening to you.

Validation is such a powerful element of conversation. Granted, it's a pretty basic concept to understand at first, but it goes deep. I say I'm scared of the dark, and you say it's okay to feel that way. Let's do something to make your experience better. Validation can literally be that easy, but when you start adding in the complexities of the real world, it can become a lot more difficult to understand.

Person A: "I can't sleep. I'm scared of the dark."

Person B: "Why? It's only dark. I thought that's something you would have grown out of by now?"

See the effect that your words can have? See how invalidating that last statement is? How's that going to make the scared person feel? How would you feel in that situation? Do you feel that way often? Do you make people feel like that in your own conversations?

These are all questions you're going to be working on throughout this book.

How to Use This Book to Master Listening

This book is designed to help you to become the best listener you can be. It's a process, and it's not something that's going to miraculously happen overnight, although we will be covering tips that deliver instant results. To make things easy, the following chapters have broken down the art of listening into all the different components that will come together to introduce the skills you need to know and the knowledge you can work with day-to-day. I'm basically saying that everything you'll read from this point on is fully actionable.

We're going to start with the basics, exploring the current state of listening in your life and highlighting some of the problems so many of us face, preventing us from actually hearing people when they are talking to us. Of course, these are the same problems that stop people from hearing us. We'll then dive into the core tips that will enable you to actively become a better listener by the end of the chapter with tips you can put into action instantly, all backed by science and psychology, of course.

Once the basics of listening have been mastered, we're then going to get into the crux of this book, exploring the essential and psychological aspects of listening, including the important, powerful methods behind validating someone, how to mindread people in order to understand and identify the true meanings in what they're saying, and then overcoming the more advanced listening problems you're going to face along the way.

You can consume the information in this book however you like. It's best to read through from front to back as special care has been taken to order the chapters that will enable you to lay a solid foundation to build your skills and understanding before moving on to the more advanced teachings. However, I understand that sometimes you may want a little teaser of the good stuff and see where this book is heading, so feel free to dive in and see what's in store.

That being said, when you're ready, let's dive into the art of listening. Use this book as the key to open a new door in your life to a world of better relationships, deeper understanding, and ultimately more meaningful connections with the people in your life.

Chapter One - Never Has the World Been Louder, Yet No One Is Listening

"When people talk, listen completely. Most people never listen." Ernest Hemingway

I've always been a firm believer that very few people out there in the world are bad people, but instead, the world is full of people simply trying to do the best they can. Before starting this chapter, I went for a mindful walk, but while waiting for the kettle to boil to make my first coffee of the day, I ended up diving into the rabbit hole they call Twitter. Of course, whether you're a user or not, you'll have heard the complaints that Twitter is a platform notorious for people all over the world shouting into the ether, slamming down their points of view in the most aggressive fashions, and becoming keyboard warriors to further their causes.

Look at any highly-viewed post (especially the posts that news websites share), and you'll see examples of this everywhere. Yet, while there are so many people talking and sharing their opinions and perspectives, it's blatantly obvious that nobody is listening to anyone else. And this is just one place. Throughout the modern world, it feels as though everyone is talking all the time.

The air is always filled with chatter, but nobody is listening to it.

Even in your own life, there are plenty of good people who have your best interests at heart, from your parents and romantic partners to your friends and coworkers. All of these groups of people would want to help you during a time of need. This is what I mean by the good intentions are there, and there are few bad people, but that doesn't mean that they have the skills and know-how to actually give you what you need, and few can resolve problems properly.

Here's an example.

Let's say you're feeling low for whatever reason, say you've lost your job, and you need a little support to get you back on your feet. Are you going to turn to someone? What do they say? Do they listen to how you're feeling, or do they feed you the generic "Don't worry, it will get better in time" line? Does this kind of advice make you feel listened to, or are they going through the motions?

Perhaps you've tried speaking out in the past, but because you don't feel listened to or understood, you've convinced yourself that it's easier to stay quiet. I'm not saying your friends or partners are bad people. I am saying that they, like the vast majority of society, lack the essential communication skills they need to listen properly. For many people, it's not that they don't want to help. It's that they don't really know how.

If people aren't listening to you in such a way, then the chances are that you're not listening to them either. Switch the roles of the example and think about what you would say. Personally, all of this is a heartbreaking realization.

I want to be the person that someone else I care about a lot can come to for help whenever they need it. I want to be reliable. I want to do what I can to help others. I want to understand and connect with other people and enjoy the meaningful relationships that stem from these experiences.

So, all of this begs a very important question: Why do we all suck at listening?

Why We Suck at Listening

Well, there are several ways to look at this, but the first question to ask that will take you to the root of the cause is to ask: When have you ever been taught how to listen properly?

Maybe in school? Not really. When I was in school, I was told to just sit in my chair and remain quiet. If anyone in the class made a noise or spoke to someone else, the teacher would just tell us off and reaffirm that we needed to remain quiet while she spoke. This means that even from a young age, we're being told that the act of listening isn't to actually listen and hear what the other person is saying with the intent to understand them and their message, but it's simply to remain quiet while someone else is speaking and await our chance to speak to share our perspectives or answers.

These aren't good habits for later in life.

These kinds of teachings we learn from a young age build momentum through our lives. As Mark Shrayber, a lifestyle blogger, writes,

"When we are taught about listening, it's often presented as a passive skill, something you have to do while you allow your eyes to glaze over, your mind to drift, all as you simply wait for your opportunity to speak again."

Waiting for the opportunity to speak again. When written like this, does this really sound like the definition of listening? Of course it doesn't, yet this is what so many of us do. Don't worry if that resonated because it defines the large majority of people and the extent of our listening skills. Fortunately, active listening is a skill that can be learned, practiced, and mastered, which is what this book is about!

That's how this book works. We're going to highlight the issues with listening, becoming aware of bad communication habits so we can undo them, and then replace them with better, more productive listening habits that help you make stronger connections with the people in your life.

Here are some of the main reasons why you may find it so hard to listen and the obstacles you may be facing unconsciously.

- You are too lost in your thoughts.

- You are not actively paying attention to the other person.

- You are distracted by someone or something else.

- You are held back by your preconceived judgments on the person or conversation topic.

- A lack of comprehensive understanding (i.e., not understanding context or language used within a conversation).

- You have a short attention span.

Reading through this list, many of these points sound bad, but many of them simply come down to the way of the world that we have been born into.

For example, over 48.1% of people have a smartphone. In the Western world, that translates to pretty much everyone being distracted by pings and notifications all the time. From the moment we wake up to the moment we go to sleep. Just constant pinging and being connected. This degree of distraction is a huge obstacle to active listening.

On top of this, statistics show that attention spans have shrunk by over 50% over the last ten years (2007–2017). Whereas a child could have an average attention span of twelve minutes back in 1998, this has shrunk to just five minutes in 2008. Guess what? As of 2017, the average for people under eighteen is now just a measly eight seconds. This is why TV and online advertisements, social media videos, and so on are all so short in duration. Snapchats and TikToks are seven seconds long because app developers know this is all we have the attention span for.

What I'm saying is that a lot of the problems you're dealing with are problems that everyone is dealing with, and it's a bit of a self-perpetuating cycle. We scroll down our social media feeds, spending less than a second on each image, which shrinks our attention spans, which affects our listening, and it's just getting worse. Casey Neistat, the YouTuber and filmmaker, summed it up perfectly.

He asked his viewers to imagine sitting in front of a television screen and scrolling through the channels but spending less than a second on each channel. Could you find what you're looking for in that time? No? That's exactly what we're doing when we fast-scroll down our Facebook timelines. You see my point?

Depressing? Perhaps. Inspirational? Definitely. With this information, I'm hoping you'll be inspired and motivated enough to become aware of your own habits and ultimately do something about them.

Furthermore, Listen.org also has a ton of helpful statistics that show why we're such terrible listeners, coupling it with what I listed out above. There are statistics like:

- The average person can listen to around 175 words per minute but can think at 2,000 words per minute, so of course, it's easy to get lost in and distracted by our thoughts while listening.

- Most people will only remember 50% of what has just been said to them.

- Over the long term, the average person will only remember around 20% of what has been spoken to them.

- Around 70% of our time at work is spent communicating with other people, and this is broken down into 45% of the time listening, 30% talking, 16% reading, and 9% writing things down.

To cut a long story short, all of this combined clearly shows we're all suffering from sensory overload, and we're all exhausted from it. We spend so much time listening and consuming information from so many sources, all while forgetting more than half of it in the long term anyway. Then, top that with our overactive minds, it's no wonder that proper listening is so difficult.

But, as I've said, it's possible to develop new listening skills and break yourself free from the cycle that so many of us are stuck in, and with so many great reasons to do so.

The Benefits of Proper Active Listening

There's a reason you picked up this book, but if it all seems like doom and gloom so far, don't worry, it's really not. I remember reading those statistics for the first time and being like, *Wow, this is where we've got to?* but I soon switched my mindset to remember that with this knowledge, you're able to move forward. It's like a journey. You're marking on the map where you are now (not a great listener), highlighting where you want to go (to becoming a better listener), and now we're plotting the route of how you're going to get there.

But before we leave, what are you going to find at the other end? What are the benefits of listening? Fortunately, there is a lot to consider.

- You'll be able to make better decisions because you'll have more information to work with in any given situation because you've listened to all sides of a story or learned new data from other people.

- You'll be able to see the hidden messages and agendas behind what someone is saying, potentially uncovering underlying issues in people's lives, and can tell when people are lying to you.

- You'll have better, deeper, more connected relationships with the people in your life, meaning you'll be happier, more fulfilled, and more satisfied with your life and can provide proper support when needed.

- You have more substantial and more fulfilling conversations, even when engaged in small talk.

- You'll become a far more compassionate, empathetic, and grateful person because you'll be appreciating the contributions other people have made far more often.

As you can see, the benefits can tap into every area of your life. Psychologist Carl Rogers writes about how active and deep listening is at the heart of every healthy relationship, and for so many reasons. You read any article or book on how to have better relationships, and the number one tip always refers to learning how to communicate better.

Studies show that listening and showing someone you understand what they're saying makes them more open and more democratic in their future conversations with you. Listening also naturally makes people less defensive. Listening and making attempts to understand someone also strengthens relationships because it shows you care about them and what they have to say. This, in turn, makes them more inclined to listen to you back.

All of this is backed by science. In a 2001 study, Willard Harley, a psychologist, discovered the top ten most important elements that people want when focusing on intimate relationships. Among the top ten results was the need for *intimate conversation,* which boiled down to people wanting their partners to give and receive undivided attention while communicating.

Take a moment to think about your current relationships with people who mean the most to you. Remember times when you've been arguing and how uncompassionate and unconnected you feel from your partner at the heat of the interaction? Now reimagine those times turning out the way you would want them to turn out. Conversations that are typically arguments but instead are conversations with little to no judgments, more democracy, openness, and less defensive attitudes. How much stronger would your relationships be if that's how your conversations went? How much more productive and beneficial would your conversations be?

It's all possible through the practice of listening and mindfully trying to understand other people. By now, I think it's safe to say that we get where we're at as listeners now and what is possible by actively listening, so I'm going to cut myself short and start moving into the meat of this book. Just like all the top blogs and books say, listening is so important, so now I think it's about time to dive into how to do it better.

Once you're ready to start making big positive changes in your life, it's time to turn the page and take that first step on your new journey.

Chapter Two - The Psychology of Listening

"The most basic of all human needs is to understand and be understood. The best way to understand people is to listen to them." Ralph Nichols

What is listening?

Is it to hear the words that someone else is saying? Is it to nod politely and await your turn for speaking? The dictionary definition of listening is perhaps a surprising one, which reads:

To give attention with the ear closely for the purpose of hearing.

A more modern definition would include being able to listen with the intent to understand what is being said. We can all hear words sent our way, but the real skill of listening comes from being able to understand the message of what's being said. This chapter is all about understanding the basic skills needed to listen and understand, so by the end of this chapter, you're already going to be well on your way to becoming a better listener.

Selective Hearing: The Downfall of Listening

The science behind the psychology of listening is one of the most interesting fields of science I've ever looked into, which is where we're going to start, and the first stop is to the station of selective hearing. Chances are, you've been in a situation where you've said something to someone, but it feels as though they're only picking out the certain bits that they want to hear. This is commonly referred to as "selective hearing."

Here's an example. You might have had a conversation with your partner that goes along the lines of:

Person A: "Hey, there's a show happening next week with that actor I like. Do you think you'd be interested in getting some tickets?"

Let's imagine the partner is sitting in a chair playing on their phone. They might grunt, or half-respond, or could perhaps ignore the statement completely. This isn't done specifically to be malicious, but rather they are listening, but their selective hearing has decided that because they're not interested in going to the show, they just don't want to respond.

However, in the same sentence, Person A could say:

Person A: "Hey, there's a show happening next week with that actor I like. Do you think you'd be interested in getting some tickets? We could get some for the football game while we're there."

Suddenly, Person B puts their phone down and engages in conversation because they picked up on a subject that they're interested in. I can't tell you how many times I've been there.

Of course, this isn't a healthy way to converse with your loved ones, but you'll be amazed at how often this kind of listening occurs in day-to-day conversations. If you're having an in-depth conversation with someone, you'll start to notice that many people only respond to the topics of conversation they care about. This makes sense, to a degree. The problem is that if you say something important, and they selectively hear but a little of what you said, you're going to unconsciously feel misunderstood and not listened to, and you'll end up becoming defensive. Ultimately, from here, the conversation is doomed.

To be a well-rounded listener, you need the ability to focus and understand everything that's being said, not just picking out the bits you care about. Remember the example conversation I shared in the introduction about my partner wanting to leave her job? By only responding with concerns of money and bill paying, I'm selectively hearing the part of the conversation that I care about and ignoring everything else, including what matters to my partner.

To overcome issues and conflicts like this happening, you need to branch out to switch up your style of listening. Fortunately, according to science and psychology, there are 27 unique types of listening that you can dive into and try for yourself (sometimes 33, depending on the research you're referring to).

Let's cover them below for clarity's sake, but don't feel like you need to remember them all right away. We'll break it down further afterward.

The 27 Types of Listening

Type of Listening	Description
Active Listening	Listening to someone with your full attention while actively moving to encourage further speaking (such as nodding your

	head) and physically showing you're interested.
Appreciative Listening	Actively listening to someone while looking for opportunities to praise and share an appreciation for what is being said. For example, listening to an athlete talking about running and then giving them praise for their skill.
Attentive Listening	Showing active attention to someone, making sure to listen to all words and inflections.
Biased Listening	Listening to someone, but only through your own personal bias and preconceived judgments you already have.
Casual Listening	Listening without displaying true interest, but actual levels of attention can vary a lot.

Comprehension Listening	Listening with a solid intent to understand and learn more from the person speaking.
Content Listening	Listening with a solid intent to understand and learn more from the person speaking (same as above).
Critical Listening	Listening with the intent to criticize, evaluate, or judge what someone is saying.
Deep Listening	Listening to someone very intently to understand them, their words, personality, motives, goals, and motivations.
Dialogic Listening	Listening with the intent to ask questions to seek a deeper understanding of what someone is saying.
Discriminative Listening	Listening for something specific while dismissing and ignoring everything else you can hear,

	such as trying to listen out for a car or someone crying.
Empathetic Listening	Listening with the intent of understanding the feelings behind what someone is saying.
Evaluative Listening	Listening with the intent to criticize, evaluate, or judge what someone is saying (same as Critical Listening).
False Listening	Pretending to listen to someone, but more often than not just caught up in your own thoughts.
Full Listening	Listening with the full and honest intent to listen and understand what someone is saying. This means being active in seeking meaning in their words.
High-Integrity Listening	Listening with a concern for what the other person is saying.

Inactive Listening	Similar to false listening, pretending to listen and give attention.
Informative Listening	Listening to understand and get meaning from what is being said.
Initial Listening	Listening to the first points shared and then having the intention to interrupt.
Judgmental Listening	Same as critical and evaluative listening, but usually with negative intent. Typically have preconceived biases that affect the listening ability.
Partial Listening	Listening some of the time, but more engaged with thinking or daydreaming.
Reflective Listening	Listening to a conversation and then actively repeating back what the other person said.

Relationship Listening	Listening with the intent to emotionally support or build a relationship with the other person.
Sympathetic Listening	Listening with the intent to focus on the other person's feelings plus concern for their overall well-being.
Therapeutic Listening	Listening with the intent to understand the emotions of someone and to act empathetically towards them.
Total Listening	Listening with the maximum amount of attention it is possible to give someone, all with the intent to seek actual meaning through what is being said.
Whole-Person Listening	Listening with the intent to not only understand what is being said but also to understand the person, personality, and

	feelings of who is speaking on an individual level.

Phew! That's a lot to take in.

Remember, you don't need to remember all these different listening types, especially since you'll see that many tie in with each other or mean the same thing. However, you should have a deeper understanding of how many different layers to listening there are and how going into any conversation with different intentions will dramatically affect the outcome of the interaction.

The art of getting better at listening is literally about that. It's about being mindful as you go into your conversations and thinking, *What kind of listener do I want to be going into this conversation?* and then proceeding with control, rather than acting mindlessly while on unconscious autopilot.

Let's say, for example, you're talking with a Trump supporter, but you don't support Trump yourself.

It can be so easy to engage in judgemental and critical listening because you already have your beliefs about Trump and how you see Trump supporters act. Instead of hearing the other person, you're just waiting for the opportunity to tear apart what they're saying. Imagine you went into such a conversation with the intent to sympathetically listen or deep listen. Imagine trying to understand the person on an individual and personal level. Imagine how differently the conversation can go and what relationships and progress can form from this.

I'm not saying you need to listen and become friends with everyone you meet. Far from it. Active listening is all about achieving a beneficial outcome where you can actually learn and become a better, more rounded, more compassionate, and more educated person who can make deep and meaningful decisions, connections, and relationships with people when you want to.

Again, there's a lot of listening types to understand there, so we're going to break it all down a little further into just four of the most important types of listening, and these are the ones you're going to want to remember moving forward.

Appreciative Listening

When you listen to something to enjoy what you can hear. You could be listening to a TED Talk for fun while getting educated. You could be listening to someone talk passionately about something they're interested in, such as your friend talking about their vacation or their new business ideas. You could be listening to music. You could be watching a movie or listening to stand-up comedy. You could be listening to someone you're on a video call with.

All in all, appreciative listening means you're listening because you enjoy listening.

Comprehensive Listening

This is all about listening to understand. When you watch the news or listen to a teacher, you are comprehensively listening. You actively listen to absorb as much topical information as you can, but this is considered more difficult than most other kinds of listening because it becomes a conscious effort to listen and understand information that you don't already know.

Critical Listening

This form of listening is all about taking on new information to find out more and evaluate what is being said to you. This ranges from someone in a shop trying to sell you a new smartphone to your friend sharing their medical test results with you, and then you want to find out more about what happens next. This listening type is all about evaluating the content and making judgments to form your own opinion.

Empathetic Listening

This kind of listening is all about listening with concern and empathy for the other person and their well-being. If someone is going through a hard time and needs support, this is the kind of listening you'll try to give. You'll try putting yourself in the other person's shoes, and you'll give them your full attention, rather than trying to speak yourself. This kind of listening is all about understanding others.

These are the main types of listening, and you're definitely going to want to put effort into remembering these because they will come up the most. Go back to my first example conversation from the introduction and apply it to yourself.

Your partner has just told you they hate their job and they're looking for an out. What kind of listening are you going to apply here?

You could be critical, but it's clear they're not really looking for judgment. You could be appreciative, but the conversation won't move forward unless you're a bit sadistic and enjoy listening to others talking about how much they hate parts of their lives. These listening types are not really what you're looking for. Instead, if you apply comprehensive and empathetic listening, you're much more likely to make your partner feel understood, and you'll actually understand how they're feeling and why.

Once the conversation progresses and starts to move through the initial emotional stage, you can implement critical listening as you explore new ideas of what your partner can do next and how they can resolve the situation.

Should they stay where they are or look for something else? What are the issues you'll need to work through financially? What is your partner looking for? Those are all evolved conversations that require some degree of judgment, but it stems from you starting with the comprehensive listening type first.

Finally, it's worth mentioning that all four of the listening types we've listed above are forms of *Active Listening*. This means to show the person you're speaking with that you're intently listening and giving them your full attention, rather than just half-heartedly listening.

The Two Final Approaches to Listening

Just to make things even more complicated (only joking!), there are two other listening types you'll need to be aware of before we move forward. I bet you didn't think there were this many kinds of listening, right? If you find it easier to remember these two listening techniques instead of remembering all the others, then feel free to make these types your primary focus in future conversations until you get the hang of them.

Listening to Respond

This is the typical approach to listening that most people take.

You've done it to others, and others will have done it to you. Listening to respond is the type of listening when you're in a conversation with someone, and instead of listening to what they are saying, you already have what you want to say in mind, and you're simply waiting for them to finish. This is so you can jump in and have your say, or you may even interrupt to share your point. We spoke about this listening type earlier.

There are obvious downsides to this approach. You won't understand the person you're listening to, but more importantly, it's incredibly obvious to the other person. Once they notice, they become defensive and won't listen to you. Then, the whole conversation ends up going nowhere.

Listening to Understand

The polar opposite of listening to respond, this kind of listening involves letting go of everything you want to say and truly listening to the other person using the approaches and methods we've explored above. This is the most productive form of listening since it provides all the benefits we've described.

In the following chapters, I'm going to show you how to combine everything you've just learned into one powerful learning strategy, but hopefully, you've got a clear understanding as to just how deep the psychology of listening goes from a scientific standpoint.

However, you don't need to know all the ins and outs yourself. Of course, you can if you want to, but having a basic understanding, for now, is enough to move forward. As a recap for the most important aspects:

- Always make sure you're listening to understand others, not just waiting to force your point of view.

- Active listening is the best kind of listening.

- You can be mindful of different styles of listening in different situations by asking yourself what the best outcome of the conversation will be and deciding what the other person needs.

Chapter Three - How to Be a Better Active Listener 101

"The first duty of love is to listen." **Paul Tillich**

Ready for the crux for this book? Good, because we're here, and we're heading in fast.

By now, you should know everything about the science and psychology of listening. In other words, what it is, what true listening requires, and a *ton* of different listening types. But while you have the information on what listening is, the methods themselves don't explain *how* to do it, which is what we're going to explore in this chapter.

We'll start with basic listening skills that you need to know as your foundation for becoming a better listener, and then we'll move on to some more advanced tactics. This will be an intense chapter that includes everything you need to know, so feel free to take it a section at a time!

Bringing Awareness to Yourself (It All Starts with You!)

First things first, you need to be aware of yourself and how you show up in conversations.

When it comes to self-improvement of any kind, it all starts with, well, yourself, and the same applies when you're mastering the art of listening.

Here are some powerful tips you can start with that will immediately improve your ability to listen. This is going to be a tip-heavy chapter, so feel free to take it in stages or even bookmark this page, so you can come back at any time to refresh your memory on existing skills you've learned, or to learn new ones!

Realizing Your Judgements and Biases

What do you think about the current state of politics? How do you feel about Hollywood? What are your thoughts on the Royal Family? What are your concepts of Wall Street, the health of the environment, and Nikki Minaj?

The first thoughts that come to your mind on these topics are your judgments and biases towards them, and they can hold you back from listening properly. Here's an example:

Marie and Kyle have been married for a few years. One day, they are driving to the zoo. Kyle believes himself to be a great driver, and as Marie drives, she hesitates at a roundabout, whereas Kyle would have claimed the free space. Kyle comments with the aim of advising Marie to be a more confident driver, but Marie says it was fine and smiles at him.

Later, the couple is talking about what happened, and the conversation gets heated, and Kyle ends up getting angry and making an aggressive comment that he later regrets.

The problem with this kind of common conversation is that Kyle doesn't know (or maybe he does and doesn't apply the knowledge) the fact that her past ex-partners have demeaned Marie for not doing things right in her life, whether that's driving, cooking, cleaning, or just living her life.

At the same time, Kyle was bullied in school and made to feel powerless, and now unconsciously seeks validation for the topics he does know about—in this case, his ability and knowledge when it comes to driving.

Both Kyle and Marie have preconceived biases and ideals that affect the direction of the conversation. Marie's past experiences and bias make Kyle's friendly advice feel like piercing criticism. Marie's reluctance to learn from the criticism makes Kyle feel like his knowledge of driving is invalid and puts him on the defensive.

Now, you're certainly not able to control other people's biases, but you *can* control your own by being mindful of your own automatic and unconscious thoughts and feelings whenever they arise. If Kyle gives advice and Marie shuts it down, he needs to develop the ability to recognize the defensive feelings that come up from him being triggered. Suppose he can recognize them as being triggering rather than being consumed emotionally. In that case, he can voice these concerns with Marie and have a much more therapeutic conversation, rather than the aggressive outburst it later leads to.

These automatic responses that we feel towards everything are known as thought patterns, and you don't need to feel bad about having them because we all do. The trick is to become aware of what they are, perhaps through journaling, meditation, or even counseling if your thoughts are based on past traumas (like Kyle's bullying and Marie's ex-boyfriend problem), and then working through them, ensuring your negative patterns can turn positive.

Some considerations to remember here include:

- Learning to recognize a judgment, bias, or negative thought pattern when it arises.

- Write preexisting thought patterns down to remember them and bring more focus to them later.

- Including someone on your self-discovery journey to help you identify your less obvious patterns.

- Recording your reactions to conversations or events (writing or video).

- Try new positive reactions the next time you're in a similar conversation or situation where you want to let go of an old thought pattern.

Piece all this together, and you'll be able to go into any conversation with an open mind with the very real ability to learn and listen to others. Here's one more example to bring it home.

Let's say you hate social media. You dislike everything about it and think the world is better off without it. Someone starts talking to you about a fundraising campaign that happened on Instagram. However, as soon as they mention Instagram, you shut down and think, *I don't want to hear this because Instagram is an awful platform,* and it's a horrible conversation where everyone gets invalidated.

On the flip side, you may first have the thought that Instagram is a horrible platform, but you instead notice the judgment through awareness, and you let it go. You listen to the other person tell you about an amazing fundraising project and instead say something like, "Well, I don't use Instagram, but that sounds like an amazing project. If I give you the money, can you donate for me?"

See how different the conversation can be by dropping your judgments and listening?

Acknowledging Your Expectations

Whenever you have a conversation, you're going to be affected by your conditioning and will have expectations that dictate how you listen, just like you do with your judgments. Think about situations like going into a job interview, and you're so nervous because you simply believe it's going to go terribly. It's these expectations that will hold you back from listening properly. In this case, this will certainly ruin the job interview and turn your thoughts into a self-fulfilling prophecy.

I use the Trump supporter and anti-Trump example a lot, but that's because it was so relevant over the last few years.

Whenever these two types of people go "against" each other (especially in examples captured on video), these people will not listen to each other because their preconceived expectations prevent them from being open to what the other person has to say. It's these expectations that prevent any real, productive conversations from taking place with the potential for a positive outcome.

It's important to be aware and mindful of your own expectations and preconceptions that could be stopping you from being a proper listener in your own life. Perhaps someone at work did something stupid once, and you've always seen them as a bit of an idiot because of it. This stops you from talking to them and prevents you from accessing any of the opportunities they could bring into your life.

The same goes for your parents, partners, children, coworkers, and basically anyone you know or could meet. Some top tips to remember here to overcome your expectations include:

- Keeping a journal and writing down the thoughts whenever you have an expectation pop up.

- Making a list of all the expectations you have with different people in your life. This works because writing down your thoughts helps you focus on them more, thus making it easier to identify when they come up. When you notice them pop up, you can let them go and focus properly.

- Be active in discovering your conditioning by giving yourself keywords like money, language, immigrants, politics, religion, and the names of people in your life. Write down whatever comes to mind, and you'll soon discover how you feel and what you can learn to let go of.

- Whenever you feel an expectation or bias come into your mind when talking to someone, take a moment to breathe and let it go.

I was speaking to a friend of mine a few years back, and he started talking about his spiritual journey and how he was getting into ideas like chakras and astral projection. As we walked, he asked me what I thought, and the first thing that came to mind was how it's all spiritual rubbish and wasn't real. I believed it was false hope and that kind of thing.

However, instead of just jumping to my conditioned way of thinking and responding mindlessly, I said something along the lines of:

"You know, the first thing that came to mind was how that sounds like nonsense, but I'm not sure whether that's just because I have no experience in it. Tell me more about it, and I'll try and see through that train of thought."

This is all that needs to be said in a situation like this. Let's say your partner wants to go and try a new diet. You can say that you agree or disagree with the diet they're choosing to try, but this is just your preconceived expectation since the chances are you know nothing about it. Let your partner know this and say you're going to work on being open-minded and seeing how it goes.

The truth is, as a human being, you know practically nothing. What you don't know is almost always more important than what you do know. To quote a famous motivational speaker, you don't know enough. If you did, then your life and the lives of everyone around you would be where you want them to be.

Accept this notion, and you open up a whole new way of living in the world.

Practice Your Mindfulness Skills

A lot of everything we've spoken about so far, and easily one of the most actionable pieces of advice any listening guide or expert can give you is to be present in your conversations. This means to give the other person your full attention, and you can do this by actively improving your mindfulness skills. To be mindful is to be aware of your thoughts and in control of your attention.

With human attention spans now averaging less than that of a goldfish, you're going to need to engage in a process. It's going to be hard work. Even writing this chapter, I'm constantly feeling the pull of social media and wanting to go on my phone. As I wrote the word phone, I immediately wanted to jump on Instagram or check to see if someone has texted or emailed me.

How often do you find your mind wandering in the same way, especially when you're talking to others?

I've lost count of the number of times that someone has been talking to me, and I just zone out. It could be seconds or minutes before I think, *Damn it, I have no idea what was just said or what's going on. I've been daydreaming.* Then you have to struggle to pick up where you left off.

The act of mindfulness means having the skill to notice when your mind wanders off or isn't focused fully on the conversation you're having and then gently pulling it back.

The more you practice mindfulness, the better at it you'll become, and the shorter the time frame will be that your mind allows itself to wander. Here are some tips to help you develop your mindfulness skills:

- Bring your whole heart into a moment by using your senses to stay connected to the present. What can you see, hear, smell, and touch? Your senses help you stay grounded.

- Focus on your breathing. This is a classic meditation technique, but you'll notice how even while you read this, you can focus on your breathing and the words, and all other thoughts cease to bother you. This is a great technique to use in conversations.

- Focus on the center of your hand. This works the same as the method above, but I found it much easier to put into practice. Look at your hand and place a finger in the center of your palm. Now focus on that point, as though your awareness is inside your hand.

You can remove your finger and still focus on that bit. Keep your attention there while you read or converse with someone to maintain your focus.

- Practice meditation. Sure, meditation isn't for everyone, but there's really no better way to improve your ability to stay present and focused in everything you do in life.

- Be grateful for the moment you're living in. Gratitude is such a big part of being present. If you can appreciate that your partner, someone who loves you very much, is in front of you, this is a great way to stay focused, all because you don't want to miss another moment with them.

Controlling Your Emotions (Developing Emotional Intelligence)

If someone says something and you're offended by it, stirred by it, or even motivated by it, it's so easy to lose focus in a conversation and then to start projecting those expectations and preconceptions we spoke about earlier. If you're offended, your defenses go up, and it becomes incredibly difficult to actually hear what the other person is saying.

It takes a bit of self-development to increase your emotional intelligence, which refers to your ability to notice when your emotions arise, yet still being able to control yourself to have the outcome you want. Remember, emotions are always your body's first unconscious response, and it's so easy just to let your mind wander away with them without thinking.

A great example of this is to imagine you're in a bar and you've bought your first drink after a hard week at work. A group of people walks past you, and due to lack of space, someone accidentally knocks your drink out of your hand before you even get to enjoy the first sip.

How do you respond?

There are two ways you can go. You may feel a flood of anger and irritation towards that other person. You could feel the urge to start fighting with them, projecting your anger and irritation onto them. You react solely through emotion, completely on autopilot, as you throw your weight around and try to put that other person in their place.

This is clearly not a very emotionally intelligent way to respond.

On the other hand, the other approach doesn't mean you won't still feel that same rush of irritation and anger towards the other person. How could you not? You were so looking forward to the drink, and now you can't help but feel disappointed. However, being an emotionally intelligent person, you recognize your rising emotions, take a deep breath, and wait calmly for them to settle down before continuing with your evening. You know full well that knocking your drink over was an accident.

This is the same logic you need to apply in your own conversations if you want to be an emotionally intelligent listener. Listen, watch your emotions, and then respond in the best possible way. Unfortunately, you can't just become emotionally intelligent overnight but instead, have to keep working on it. It's a lifelong journey that you'll just need to keep working at, especially as you grow and evolve as a person.

However, there are four characteristics that come together to make an emotionally intelligent person that you'll need to master. These are:

- **Being Self-Aware:** This means having the skill to recognize your own emotions as they arise and how to express them to others honestly and effectively.

- **Capable of Self-Management:** Having the skills to control your emotions and not mindlessly get carried away with them, resulting in you acting unconsciously and without control.

- **Being Socially Aware:** Being able to recognize others' emotions and pick up their non-verbal communications.

- **Capable of Having Stable Relationships:** Having the skills to communicate effectively with others, having empathy and compassion, and knowing how to interact with different people based on their own emotional intelligence.

With that in mind, these are the actionable tips you'll need to know on how to become more emotionally intelligent, thus developing these traits. Note, we're not carrying on with our list of how to be a better listener just now (although it obviously all ties together). The following points are all about how to increase your emotional intelligence.

- **Assess Where You Are Now**

Start with self-reflecting to see where you are now, basically gauging how emotionally intelligent you are. However, this first step is definitely the most challenging since it involves taking a real hard look at yourself. It's best to do this with a pen and paper, maybe a diary or journal, and just write about how you handle situations in your life.

Ask yourself these questions to help you figure out where you are:

- Do I react differently around different people?
- Do I get anxious when talking with other people?
- What feelings do I have?
- Do I get angry quickly?

- Do I have triggers with certain topics?

- Do events in my life, such as stressful events, control how I act in situations?

The whole idea here is to highlight your strengths and weaknesses so you know what to focus on and improve.

- **Learn to See Emotions in Others**

While it's important to acknowledge your own emotions in any given situation, you need to be proactive in paying attention to others and acknowledging theirs. This is predominately and initially done using your gut instinct (which we'll talk more about later).

Whenever you're speaking with someone, take a time-out to judge how the other person is feeling. You can literally use the "How are you?" small-talk question as a reminder. Listen to their answer, and then take a second or two to feel how you feel the other person is feeling. If they say they're fine, but your gut instinct says that they feel stressed, this could be an indication to dive a bit deeper.

You can always say, "I'm glad you're okay. You do look a bit stressed, though. Is everything alright?" effectively making sure you gauged their emotions correctly. This is another skill that you'll get better with as long as you're practicing it often.

- **Be Responsible for Your Actions and Decisions**

As with the spilled drink at the bar example above, a person controlled by their emotions is acting unconsciously and without control. They are careless and will make decisions they'll regret.

I know I say this as though all lack of control is negative, but it works both ways. Imagine someone who is having so much fun at a music festival and is so overwhelmed with happiness. They then decide (without control) to let go of all their inhibitions and carelessly take random narcotics offered to them because they're lost having a good time.

The chances are a situation like that won't end well, so responsibility needs to be taken for their actions. This trait is quite simple, but it takes confidence to apply it to your life.

- If you make a mistake, own it.
- If something goes wrong in your life, learn from the experience and do the best you can next time.
- Adjust your reactions when you need to.
- If you hurt someone, apologize to them.
- Let go of your ego and aim to grow and be a better version of yourself.

Only you can make it happen.

- **Be Self Disciplined and Have Self Control**

Every human being experiences a whole spectrum of emotions throughout different times in their life, and there are going to be times where you feel so emotional it feels as though you could lose control. It's during these times you'll be tested to see how far you've come on your emotional intelligence journey.

If you find yourself in a tense, heated, or stressful situation, you must learn how to take a step back and take a few deep breaths. When you feel the emotions rising inside you, the rage or the anxiousness or whatever you're feeling, these are the moments where you start to control your breathing in an attempt to settle these feelings.

Taking this time-out allows you to think properly and make the decisions you want to make, rather than acting unconsciously.

Some good practices and habits to bring into your life include doing things like taking the time to think before you speak since this gives you time to breathe and consider what you're going to say next. You can also meditate daily, as this will help you bring presence and attention to your emotions.

There are endless strategies out there that can help you be more disciplined, and all of them will affect every area of your life, not just when it comes to your listening skills. If you've ever had hopes, dreams, and aspirations you want to turn into a reality, you're going to need the discipline to get there.

I could give you the basic advice. Even if you get 1% better than you were yesterday, you're still making progress on your journey. But I'm sure you're thinking that's slow and you want more instant results. I know I sure did when I was in the same position.

Unfortunately, it doesn't happen overnight, and you will need to get better over time. There's no other way it can happen. However, you can increase your chances of succeeding by doing the following:

- Have no excuses for your behavior
- Take ownership of your decisions and your mistakes
- Forgive yourself when you mess up (and you will mess up) and try again
- Never give up
- Set yourself rewards you can only have once you've mindfully practiced this skill

- Meditate and write down what you excel at and what you can improve on daily

- **Assert Yourself**

Since following these tips and steps will enable you to become gradually more emotionally intelligent, you'll be far more in tune with your emotions and how you're feeling, which will allow you to very clearly know your wants, needs, desires, and feelings.

This means you can be assertive with people around you, which is essential if you want to be an effective communicator. You can learn how to tell people what you want and what you need from them directly, without having to beat around the bush. You can also tell people where you stand on certain topics.

Did someone say something that really angered you? Instead of flying off the handle, you'll be able to tell them how that made them feel and help them see your side of the story. Being assertive is about finding the perfect balance between being passive and being aggressive. For example:

A: "Hey. Did you see the new girl at the reception this morning? I'd love to take her home and go wild with her!"

B: "That's incredibly inappropriate and disrespectful."

A: "Oh, lighten up. I'm just trash-talking."

B: "I'm just saying you crossed a line. Think what you want, but you should have respect for others."

A: "She's not here. It doesn't matter."

B: "How would you like it if other people spoke about your daughter in the same way? Have a bit of empathy."

A: "Yeah. Okay. I see what you mean. Sorry, I wasn't thinking."

B: "It's okay. I'm glad we didn't have to fight about it."

A tense conversation. It would be very easy for people to join into a conversation like this to try and fight in with 'office banter,' although thankful it's been addressed increasingly, or to not say anything at all, despite person A clearly crossing a line.

It's actions and conversations like this that create a far more productive conversation where people are open to learning from each other rather than fighting. Some other tips you can follow for being more assertive include doing things like:

- Believing that embarking on this journey is helping you become a better version of yourself

- Saying no to things in life that don't serve or resonate with you

- Asserting yourself in small-scale conversations

- Always remaining positive towards the outcome of a situation

- Being aware of other people's feelings and their points of view

A Summary of Becoming Emotionally Intelligent

By harnessing the power of each point we've discussed, you'll be able to ultimately become a far better listener than you could imagine since you'll be so grounded and in control of yourself, no matter who you're speaking with.

There are so many benefits to developing your emotional intelligence in this way. It will truly affect every aspect of your life, from your personal relationships and career to your confidence and levels of charisma. Anyway, that was a bit of a detour. Let's return to our list of ways to become a better active listener.

- **Awareness of Your Physical Self**

Body language is a huge part of communication (research shows that it makes up around 55% of all communication, whereas verbal communication makes up just 7%), so it pays to be in control of your own body language and creating the image you want to give to other people.

I'm going to talk a whole lot more about body language in a later chapter. Still, for now, I'll cover some actionable tips you can start introducing into your conversations right now to automatically become a better listener.

- Maintain a balanced degree of eye contact. Don't just stare at people, but don't avoid eye contact altogether. Show you're listening with the amount of eye contact that feels comfortable.

- Keep your back straight and sit upright. You don't want to overdo this to seem as though you're trying to overpower the other person with confidence, but you don't want to slouch to seem bored or disconnected. Give the impression you're engaged in the conversation.

- Don't fiddle with anything or play with your hands. This sends the message you're either nervous or distracted, neither of which you want other people to think since they'll start talking to you differently.

- Use expressions. When you're talking, talk with your whole body as this will make you seem far more engaged and a part of the conversation. Use hand gestures to emphasize your points.

- Nod and smile as a sign of acknowledgment that you want the other person to keep speaking and encourage them to keep going while you're listening.

- **Awareness of Your Vocal Self**

Finally, you want to pay attention to how you're coming across while you're talking back, answering questions, and sharing your points of view. It's all well and good showing good body language, but many people will react to how you're saying what you're saying and how you're presenting yourself.

The main considerations you need to be thinking about are things like:

- The volume of your voice (are you whispering or shouting?)

- The tone of voice you have (whether you're stern, sarcastic, happy, energetic, and so on)

- What kind of inflection you place on certain words

It's always best to speak in a cool, calm, and collected fashion to portray your message if you want to be listened to.

However, there will be times when you need to speak sternly, such as if you're disciplining a child or times when you want to be hyper and excited, like when you're going to a concert with friends. It's all about the context of the conversation you're in, so be active in choosing the right kind of voice for the situation.

As you can see, for a lot of these points, it's all about taking your mind and body off autopilot and taking back control of how you communicate and how you listen to others. It's applying control in this way that you'll get the outcome you want from the conversation.

The Key Active Listening Skills You Need to Know

These are the first skills that come into play when you want to listen to someone more effectively and deeply. You can apply the following tips literally right now and see an instant improvement in your ability to communicate and listen.

Let Someone Speak without Interruption

When I started work on bettering my skills as a listener, it became shockingly apparent how much I interrupted people and how much they interrupted me. Interrupting seems to be commonplace nowadays, and reading this right now will make you so much more aware of it in your own conversations. Sorry about that. Another thing you won't be able to unsee.

You can counter this by being mindful and aware enough to let others finish everything they're saying. This way, you'll be able to get the full context out of their message, and it will make the person speaking feel as though you care about what they're saying, rather than just trying to shoehorn your perspective into the conversation.

Minimize Distractions

You can't give someone your full attention if you're distracted by other things that are going on around you. When someone starts speaking to you, put your phone down so you can't see the screen, close your book, and turn off your computer monitor. If you're talking in a loud place where you can't hear thanks to external noises, you can suggest moving to a quieter location.

It's actions like this that show you care.

Show How Much You're Paying Attention

There are plenty of ways you can use your body to not only show you're giving someone your full attention but also trick your body into actually giving someone your full attention. You can easily do this by:

- Making eye contact

- Leaning forward towards the speaker when they say something that interests you

- Nodding in agreement to points

- Saying "yes" and "uh-huh" to encourage the speaker to keep going at the appropriate points in the conversation

- Smiling to show shared humor within the conversation

Avoid Making Judgments

As soon as you're aware that you're making judgments on what someone is saying, you're taking yourself out of listening and are instead distracted by thoughts, which means you're not listening. Through practice, you'll be able to become aware of distracting, judgmental thoughts, which you can nip in the bud by reapplying your focus to listening. When you're judging, you're not listening.

This applies to your preconceived judgments and biases, as we spoke about in the last section, and if someone uses the wrong word to describe something or speaks out of context. Simple mistakes can happen, and not everyone is a brilliant communicator. If someone makes a mistake and it stops you from listening, you need to let your judgments go if you want the conversation to continue being productive.

Repeat Back What You Heard

I will speak about this point a lot more in the following chapters, but a great way to improve your listening skills is to repeat back the key points of what you just heard.

Imagine someone says something along the lines of:

> "I really love running because I feel so free and peaceful."

You can reply with something like:

> "It makes you feel free? In what way?"

It's the act of repeating the information back that not only clarifies what's being said in your own head, meaning there's much less of a chance you're going to forget it, but you're showing the other person you're genuinely taking on board what they're saying and hearing their message.

The Key Active Listening Habits You Need to Avoid

Just like there are plenty of habits and skills you can use to improve your abilities as an active listener, you should avoid the mistakes and bad habits that will make you seem like a passive listener or someone who isn't paying attention. However, by learning what they are, you'll be able to avoid them.

Rushing Someone to Finish

I've seen people who have been quite abrupt with rushing someone to finish speaking literally by saying things like "Come on, get to the point," and so on.

However, there are other more subtle ways this can happen, such as checking a watch or phone for the time or looking anywhere other than at the person who's speaking. This unconsciously makes it look like you're looking for a way out.

Rushing someone to finish will not make the other person feel listened to but will rather distract them from saying what they want to say.

Sure, there can be times when people will talk too much and won't be speaking concisely, but if you want a relationship with someone, you've got to have the respect to let them express themselves how they want to.

Changing the Subject Abruptly

Another common trait I see among people all the time.

We've all been in situations where someone is speaking about something that matters to them, and the conversation changes suddenly. This is another way of rushing the person to finish and making them believe that what they were talking about isn't relevant or cared about.

Changing the subject will shut the other person down, makes them defensive, and ultimately makes them less likely to listen to you. This is only going to cause conflict in your conversations. Here's an example that happened a week or so ago when I was visiting my parents.

I, my mother, and my father were doing the dishes after dinner. Dad's talking about how he follows the shares his bank gave him but doesn't know why he spends time doing that since he hasn't done anything with the stocks in over a decade.

Dad: "But yeah, I guess it's just a habit to check them."

Me: "Do you think it's something you would be interested in spending more time on now that you're retired?"

Mom: "Oh, what is that smell?"

From here, my dad became extremely defensive and asked my mother to repeat what he had just said, to which she couldn't answer, and an argument proceeded about not being listened to, and quite rightly too. The blatant change in subject only said my mother didn't care at all about what my father was saying, which made him defensive, and the conversation derailed.

In short, just avoid changing the subject abruptly and let people get to the end of what they're saying, simply out of the same respect you would want from other people.

Using Humor at the Wrong Times

I'm massively guilty of this one.

For a long time, humor was a big coping mechanism for me, and even when the situation wasn't funny or the topic was negative, I would still laugh or make a joke because it helped me process the information and deal with the potential awkwardness of talking about it. It wasn't even laughing in a "haha, that's funny" kind of way, but it was more of a nervous laugh.

Still, not everyone I spoke to knew that.

This was a completely unconscious response I had, and if someone didn't know me very well, the laugh could so easily be taken out of context and made to feel as though I was making a joke out of the situation. This, again, makes people feel as though I'm not listening, nor taking the situation seriously, therefore not respecting what the other person has to say.

Focusing on Small Details Rather Than Bigger Picture

It's so easy to fall into the trap of focusing on the small point of what someone is saying rather than seeing the big picture of the ideas they're sharing. I saw this all the time during my career in sales and marketing when we were brainstorming client ideas, and someone would always get hung up on the details.

An example of this could be two people discussing ideas for redecorating a living room.

A: "I'm thinking we go with a nice blue wall with maybe a mirror at the back. You see this photo? I really like the lighting the mirror helps create. It makes the color nicer."

B: "I don't really like the mirror, though. The frame isn't that nice and doesn't fit what we're going for."

In this situation, person B wasn't listening to person A. The point wasn't about the mirror being nice or something they would have, but instead, they were talking about the effect the mirror had on the room. Comments like what person B made are only going to make A feel as though they're not being listened to nor understood.

If you're able to bear all these points in mind and start applying them to your own conversations, you're going to instantly see such a big improvement in the quality of your conversations and ultimately how people talk to you, listen to you, and connect with you.

Maybe you have some bad habits when it comes to conversing. Mine included such an absence of eye contact, laughing at the wrong time, interrupting people, and it was hard to start incorporating the advice.

For example, it felt unnatural and weird to make eye contact at all, let alone for a suitable amount of time, but being aware of the changes I wanted to make and knowing that doing so would improve my relationships tenfold, I was able to introduce the positive habit into my life.

I became my own proof that the methods work.

Keep practicing and incorporating them. Like any life skill, it will take time for them to become conversational traits that you don't even need to think about, but you can only get there through experience, so don't give up!

Now we're going to dive into more advanced listening strategies that will take your conversations to a whole other level.

Chapter Four - Validation: The Key to Extraordinary Listening

"Just like children, emotions heal when they are heard and validated."- Jill Bolte Taylor

From the introduction of this book, I've spoken here and there about the aspect of validation, of course promising that we're going to dive into it in more detail. I've called it such an important aspect of conversation and effective communication that it demands its own dedicated chapter, so here we are!

Let's start with the basics.

What is validation?

There are many myths out there, the biggest one being that validation means that you just agree with someone with anything they say. That's not validation at all. That's just being agreeable.

Genuine validation is a little different. If someone says you're baking a cake the wrong way or that the Kardashians are the best thing to happen to the US since sliced bread, validating that person and their opinion doesn't mean you're agreeing with those ideas and taking them as facts. *That's validating someone's ego.*

True communicative validation is all about accepting the person you're speaking with as the *person* they are, which means listening to them and accepting that what they're saying is their belief. This is how you make someone heard and feel listened to, and this is how true relationships are formed.

You can disagree with absolutely everything someone is saying, but you can still validate them.

Here's an example for clarity.

My father was a very conservative man.

He worked every day of his life, ran his own business with ten or so employees, and made a good, stable income to support his family. My father despised paying taxes. He lived in Canada and paid taxes there. Canada also has a welfare system, but he hated that his taxes were paying the welfare of people he thought "simply couldn't be bothered to work" and were leeching off the system.

Now, as most of us know, the welfare system is incredibly complicated. While there are certainly people who take from the system when they don't need to, statistics show that the vast majority of people on the system are on it because they need the support it offers.

If you have a mother who's newly single and has two children, of course, the state is going to help her get back on her feet. When she can work, she'll earn, support her children, pay her taxes back in, and once her children grow up, having been supported by the state, they'll be able to make their own contributions, and so the system continues to cycle.

The subject is infinitely complex, but whenever my father had his yearly tax bill notification come through the post, we would have the same conversation. He was adamant he was being ripped off, and there was nothing he could do about it. I don't necessarily agree with his point of view that the welfare system is a con for the reasons above—far from it. But, I can see why my father would hate to pay 30% tax on everything he earned. That's a pretty decent chunk of income, especially when he was only slightly over the higher tax bracket.

Because I validated my father whenever we spoke about this situation, we still maintained a positive, nurturing, and deep relationship through the time he was alive. We were also close and always got along, even if we had differing opinions on certain subjects, such as paying taxes.

We still listened to each other and accepted each other for who we were.

Think about this on the flip side.

How many people do you know who are so stuck in their ways of thinking, they don't want to hear anyone else's opinion? It's impossible to have a meaningful, satisfying relationship if you can't listen to the people in them and hear what they're saying. The most powerful way you can prove that you are doing these things is through validation.

If you're looking for a powerful visual example, head over to YouTube and type in *Jordan Peterson calmly dismantles feminism* (Jordan Peterson, *Daily Politics Show*, 2018).

This isn't about whether or not you agree with the video's content, but it's a fantastic example of how terrible communication is in the modern age, especially when it comes to controversial conversations like race discrimination and politics. Watch the video and see how the two presenters aren't listening to Jordan speak whatsoever, nor validating anything he says, but how he does.

It's mind-blowing to me how poor their listening skills are, and these are people who are supposed to be interviewing someone but instead take the opportunity to shoehorn in their own points of view and try to catch him out.

This may be an extreme case, but this is exactly what so many of us do in our own relationships with the people we love. We hear what we want to hear. We make assumptions based on certain parts of what someone is saying so that their words fit our own narratives, and we drive home our perspectives rather than developing a proper conversation.

By learning how to validate the people you're speaking to, you'll improve your own listening skills and make the other person feel heard, making them less defensive and more open and honest with you, creating a meaningful relationship in the process.

So, how do you do it? Fortunately, there's a six-step guide that details everything you need to know.

The Six-Step Guide to Validating Someone

The following actionable process I'm going to share has been highlighted over the years by psychologists and researchers like Dr. Marsha Linehan, the creator of dialectical behavior therapy (known as DBT). Top life coaches also recommend this process, and authors like Patrick King in his book *How to Listen, Hear, and Validate.*

You don't need to memorize every step of this process, but instead, work on one step at a time, apply the teachings to your conversations, and build up your conversational capabilities. With experience, you'll become far better at validating others, and you'll see the results almost instantly.

When I first came across these techniques, I read about them on the train to work, and with the information fresh in mind, I applied the methods when I arrived and found the changes were immediate. That's how powerful these subtle changes in your behaviors can be. So, let's get into the steps.

Step One - Be Present

First and foremost, you have to be present in your conversations. We've spoken about this already, but it's just as important as the rest of these steps. As a quick recap, you need to:

- Give someone your full attention
- Listen to what they're saying
- Be mindful of the words and tone someone is using

If you're playing on your phone or working on a computer, you're distracted and not present, and you won't be able to fully engage with any of the following steps.

Imagine how much better your conversations with your loved ones would be if you gave them your full attention with this step alone. This is especially important during tough conversations. If someone is sharing a problem or negative emotions with you, and you're not sure how to deal with what you're being told, perhaps they're even shouting at you aggressively, this can make you uncomfortable, and you'll want to distract yourself.

This means you'll begin to lack presence, thus invalidating the person you're speaking with, and the conversation will begin to spiral downwards.

Here's an example.

A: "I'm so mad at you right now. You had no right to go and spend money on that account without asking me. I feel like you're betraying me or don't believe we're a team, and you can approach me to talk about big decisions like this."

B: "But I wanted to surprise you. I know it's a lot of money, but I just wanted to make things nicer."

A: Can you see how betrayed this would make me feel? Imagine if I did the same to you. How would you feel?"

B feels ashamed and starts to look at the ground, playing with their hair, fiddling with things on the table, and not looking at person A. Person A becomes more infuriated.

A: "What do you have to say then? Are you even listening?"

It's a hard conversation for both A and B. When B gets distracted and loses presence in the conversation, person A immediately gets defensive, and the conversation escalates to unproductive levels of aggression. Sure, it may not be right for person A to be so aggressive, but you can't control other people. You can only ever control your own actions and responses.

Let's say person B was practicing being present.

A: "I'm so mad at you right now. You had no right to go and spend money on that account without asking me. I feel like you're betraying me or don't believe we're a team, and you can approach me to talk about big decisions like this."

B: "But I wanted to surprise you. I know it's a lot of money, but I just wanted to make things nicer."

A: "Can you see how betrayed this would make me feel? Imagine if I did the same to you. How would you feel?"

Person B maintains eye contact and remains present in the conversation, even though they're mindful that they want to look away and disconnect from the conversation.

B: "Yes. I can see what you're saying, and I'm putting myself in your shoes. I would feel the same."

Person A takes a deep breath, understanding that they have been listened to and understood.

A: "I'm glad you can see how I'm feeling. I'm sorry I shouted. I just felt really intense about it all."

As you can see, from one change in the conversation, just by remaining present, the entire direction and outcome of the conversation changed to be far more positive than it would be before. To remain present in a conversation, here are some actionable tips to remember.

- Maintain eye contact.

- Listen with your body.

- If you feel yourself wanting to do something else, become aware of that thought and choose an alternative action.

- Keep a diary where you make notes on conversations you had throughout the day and highlight times where you weren't present and times you were. This will help you focus on being more present in future conversations.

- Meditate to increase your mindfulness abilities and sense of presence in conversations.

- Start the conversation off positively using your tone and language. If you're not going into a conversation positively, you're going to want to get out as quickly as possible and thus will end up looking for a way out and are, therefore, no longer present.

Step Two - It's All About Reflection

Taking step one into account, you're present, and you're listening to the people you're speaking with. You're taking on their ideas and hearing what they say. From here, the next step is to be reflective of what you've just heard. This is the part of the process where you need to be able to hear what someone is saying and look past your own personal beliefs, judgments, and biases.

There are plenty of ways you can do this, such as repeating back what someone has said to ensure what you've heard is correct, and you've taken on board what the other person has said and, most importantly, have understood the message the way it was intended.

That's not always easy. Sometimes people you'll speak with will have very valid points, but due to poor communication skills, there can be a lot of rambling that you need to sift through, which is why it's important to reflect on what the person has said, provide them with a summary (in your own words), and get to the point of what's being spoken about before formulating your own response.

Take the spending money example from the last step.

A: "I'm so mad at you right now. You had no right to go and spend money on that account without asking me. I feel like you're betraying me or don't believe we're a team, and you can approach me to talk about big decisions like this."

B: "But I wanted to surprise you. I know it's a lot of money, but I just wanted to make things nicer."

A: "Can you see how betrayed this would make me feel? Imagine if I did the same to you. How would you feel?"

B: "Yes. I understand you feel betrayed because I went behind your back and made a big decision without discussing it with you. If you did that to me, I would feel the same."

See how person B reflects back on what person A said, puts the message into their own words, and repeats it back, accurately reflecting the message and therefore validating what's been said? There is no doubt in person A's mind that they haven't been listened to nor understood, which will allow the conversation to progress productively.

However, understandably, this is person B agreeing with what person A said and is understood. If greater clarity was needed, the conversation could look something like:

A: "I'm so mad at you right now. You had no right to go and spend money on that account without asking me. I feel like you're betraying me or don't believe we're a team, and you can approach me to talk about big decisions like this."

B: "But I wanted to surprise you. I know it's a lot of money, but I just wanted to make things nicer."

A: "Can you see how betrayed this would make me feel? Imagine if I did the same to you. How would you feel?"

B: "I understand you're upset because it's a lot of money, but it was spent on both of us, more as a present for you that we can both enjoy. Can you tell me more about how you feel betrayed? If I spent the money on myself and not you, and didn't tell you, then I would understand the feelings of being betrayed. Explain just so I can understand where you're coming from properly."

With this kind of response, person B is validating the feelings of person A by basically saying, "Okay, I understand how you're feeling, and I'm not disputing you're wrong in feeling the way you do. I accept you feel the way you feel, but I still need clarity when it comes to understanding why you're thinking the way you're thinking."

Some of the best ways to be accurately reflective include:

- Repeating back a summary of what the person said in *your own* words. You're not a parrot!

- Asking thoughtful questions when you need more information on what someone has said and need more understanding.

- Matching the person's tone and inflection, positively or negatively.

Step Three - Implement Feeling Words

The next step that works hand in hand with the step above is using "feeling" words in your conversations to help you connect and understand even further.

If someone feels as though you're not really listening, understanding, nor empathizing with what they have said, this is the step that will help you overcome this conversational obstacle.

It's a shame that people living in the modern age are so disconnected from their feelings. Usually, through no fault of their own, people may have been invalidated by their parents, teachers, or peers from a young age, leading to them being emotionally disconnected from themselves as adults.

An example of this would be a child who enjoys drawing and painting. They draw and paint pictures like other children do, and naturally needing validation from their parents, the child shows them. This is a perfectly natural chain of events.

However, imagine a situation where a child paints a snail or a cat and shows their mother who is on the phone at the time. The child shows the painting and the mother, who's occupied, simply dismisses the painting, telling the child to go away because she's busy or gives a simple "Oh yes, that's great, honey."

This may seem like nothing to you or me, but from a child's perspective, when a parent is the king or queen of their world and is so dismissive, such dismissals and acts of invalidation can be devastating, especially when it happens consistently and frequently. This invalidates the child and their feelings over a long-term period.

Another example would be where a child falls over and hurts themselves. In a bid to calm the child down, the parents will say something like, "Oh, you're okay. It doesn't hurt."

See how there's such a lack of validation for how the child feels in a statement such as that? The child is thinking, *I hurt. It hurts. I want someone to make it better.*

We know as adults that falling over and hurting yourself is not so much of a big deal. Heartbreak or breaking a bone is much more painful, which is why we can dismiss the child's pain as a minor injury, yet to a child, this could be the biggest pain they're faced in their entire lives, so relatively speaking, it really does hurt.

For a parent to dismiss and actively invalidate their child in such a way will only lead to the child doubting that how they feel at any given time is valid. They believe they feel feelings that they shouldn't be feeling, as this way of thinking is how many people are as adults.

By using feeling words in your conversations, you're helping the person you're speaking with to open up about how they feel. Not only are you helping and encouraging them to express themselves because you're saying, "It's okay to talk about this because it's how you're feeling," but you're also validating how they feel because, as with step two, you're repeating back their message.

Let's head back to our example. I've highlighted the feeling words that help to validate person A's message.

A: "I'm so mad at you right now. You had no right to go and spend money on that account without asking me. I feel like you're betraying me or don't believe we're a team, and you can approach me to talk about big decisions like this."

B: "But I wanted to surprise you. I know it's a lot of money, but I just wanted to make things nicer."

A: "Can you see how betrayed this would make me feel? Imagine if I did the same to you. How would you feel?"

B: "I understand you're angry and upset because it's a lot of money, but it was spent on both of us, more as a present for you that we can both enjoy. Can you tell me more about how you feel betrayed? If I spent the money on myself and not you, and didn't tell you, then I would understand the feelings of being betrayed. Explain a little more, just so I can understand where you're coming from properly."

Person B is repeating back the exact feeling words that person A used ("betrayed" and "angry"), which validates them and then adds their own words like "upset." While person A never used the word upset, person B uses it to show they're listening and understanding how person A feels.

Of course, there's always the chance that the person you're speaking with may correct you. They may say, "No, I'm not nervous, I'm excited," or "No, that's not right. I'm not confused. I'm curious," and that's perfectly fine to be corrected as well. This is all part of having a proper conversation that will lead to productive outcomes and more meaningful relationships.

The trick here is just to use feelings words, so here are some example sentences to give you an idea of how this is possible.

- I can see that you're angry.

- I'm so happy for you! You must feel amazing right now.

- I imagine that comment from your boss was pretty hurtful.

- God, that text must have made you feel so angry.

- That's really sad.

- Wow, you must have been so happy to hear that news.

- I'm so jealous. You must have found that meal so delicious.

Some powerful invalidating feeling responses that you should avoid include statements like:

- It will be fine in the end.

- It probably could be worse, though.

- Just smile, and it will be fine.

- It will probably work out.

- I don't know why you're sad. It's not that much of a big deal.

Step Four - Discover the Context, Based on the Individual You're Talking To

Step four is the most important in your validation process because it's all about connecting with the person you're speaking with on an individual level.

It can be difficult to validate someone who you don't know because you're validating on the whim of how they are acting at that moment in time. For example, someone might be having a really bad day and have reached their breaking point, resulting in them being loud and outspoken when they are just stressed and are usually quite quiet and reserved.

On the flip side, the more you know someone and the closer you get to them, the better you'll be able to validate them because you can base your responses on their behaviors that you instinctively know. There are two key areas you'll want to think about here:

- The person's history

- The person's biology

Don't worry, when I first started learning about this process, I read those and thought, *What? This is getting way too complicated now!* but it's not as complex as you may first believe.

A really simple example of this would be someone who was scratched, bitten, or chased by a dog, even just one time, but now they really don't like being around dogs and feel really uncomfortable with them. In a situation like this, you would validate how they're feeling by saying something like, "Given your history, I can see why you don't want to come into the garden when the dog's here."

Since you've validating how they feel, you can then move on by saying something like:

"Given that the experience was ten or so years ago, you could always try and let it go. Perhaps not now, but my dog is really friendly and won't bite. Here, do you want to try to meet him slowly?"

They might say yes or no, but it doesn't matter. The point is that you're communicating effectively, showing you understand the person's concerns, but you're still progressing productively.

Back to the example.

A: "I'm so mad at you right now. You had no right to go and spend money on that account without asking me. I feel like you're betraying me or don't believe we're a team, and you can approach me to talk about big decisions like this."

Taking everything we've known now, you can really start to change up your responses by removing the first comment and jumping straight into the validation part of the conversation.

B: "I understand you're angry and upset. It's a lot of money. I justified the spending in my mind because it was spent on something we can both enjoy."

A: "I can see that."

B: "I can see why you feel this way. I remember you saying your ex-boyfriend was very controlling when it came to how you spent money and that me doing this could be very triggering. I'm sorry. I wasn't thinking about that at the time, but I can see it now."

In this example, person A and person B could be husband and wife, and since they know each other very well, they will know each other's history and why they are responding in the way they are. Person A could be very worried about money because they've had poor money management experiences in the past, or in this case, had an ex-partner who was very controlling when it came to finances. This is why they are responding in such a negative way.

The context to which someone will respond or feel in a conversation and in any given situation will obviously vary dramatically depending on the individual you're talking to, which is why you can validate them far more effectively if you know someone. If you don't know someone, then you'll just need to do the best you can.

You can do this by asking questions. If someone seems apprehensive about going into a garden with your dog, you can ask, "Are you okay? Have you had a bad experience with dogs before?"

Some tips to remember when centering someone while validating them include:

- Remembering past experiences, memories, and topics the person you're speaking with has told you about their life and how it relates to the current situation.

- Remembering that everybody has prejudices, judgments, and preconceptions on ideas and topics that can fog what they actually believe.

- Past experiences will affect people's judgments in any given situation.

- Judgments can be overcome by acknowledging them, validating them, and then offering a different alternative way forward.

- If you don't know enough about someone to know their experiences, you can ask them for clarity, but always be careful and make sure you're not crossing any typical social boundaries. You don't want to go too personal with someone you don't know. You need to build trust first.

Step Five - Create an Accepting Environment, Dismiss Judgments

When someone opens up about a situation in their life or shares their point of view, it's hard not to feel alone in how they feel. If you've ever been through a breakup and you've been telling your friends what happened, you could be so upset to the point where you're balling your eyes out, but your friends can still look fairly neutral. Even though they're supporting you, you're still going to feel as though you're the only one feeling the way you do, which is going to make you feel isolated and potentially judged.

Switch the roles around and imagine you're comforting a friend who's been through a breakup. As a listener who's supporting your friend, you want to create an environment that validates their grief and shows that you're not judging what's being said or how they're feeling.

This is known as "normalizing" and is the core element that goes into step five.

In this situation, you would say something like, "Of course you're going to feel upset. Anybody who goes through a breakup is going to feel exactly the same."

This normalizes how the person feels, but it's essential to make sure you're not following this through with something like, "You're going to be fine." It's statements like this that then invalidate how the person feels because it claims that how they are feeling now is not fine when in reality, it's perfectly acceptable. See the step above for a recap on that.

Sure, it's not nice to feel sad and upset, nor to be in a position where you're mourning a relationship, but it's perfectly normal to feel that way, and while we all know it gets better in time, that will happen when it's meant to. There's no need to rush this process. This is another example of how you can communicate in a non-accepting environment using just your words, even when you're attempting, in this case, to make someone feel better.

The best way to remember this step is by thinking about the fact you're validating someone through human experiences that everyone has. Simply put, if someone is crying because they are sad, you can validate their emotions by saying that's fine. Most people will cry when they're sad. Here are some other examples of ways you can implement step five in various situations.

- Don't worry; everyone gets stressed out and loses their cool from time to time.

- It's quite natural to be scared of bees. Lots of people are.

- Oh yes, loads of people love U2. They have millions of hits on YouTube.

- Lots of people enjoy Rick Astley.

- It's okay to feel sad. Anyone would if they were in your position.

- I would definitely be angry as well if I were in your shoes.

Step Six - Show Genuine Care and Validation

Finally, we get to step six, which is an interesting one. When I first came across the DBT process, I believed that all the steps up until here were about showing genuine care and validation for those we were listening to. What else could be said?

Well, the keyword here to remember is "genuine."

If you pretend to do any of the steps above but aren't really engaged in the conversations, and you're just following the steps because you feel like it's the right thing to do, this will come across as disingenuous, and that will cause problems in itself. Even if you know all the verbal and body language tips, you're human and can't fake them all, and it takes a lot of effort to know how to trick another person's human instinct, even if they can't put their finger on why they feel you're disingenuous.

Whenever you communicate with someone, and you're in the process of validating them, always make sure you're coming from a place where you're honest and truthful, but also authentic. If you don't really care about the person you're speaking with, that's also okay, but you need to make this known because if you just hang around and let the person open up, you're going to hurt them even more in the long term, but more on that in a moment.

Take Step Two, for example. You could so easily go into a conversation and just mimic everything they are saying to you in an emotionless way and believe that's normalizing and validating for them, but it's not. You'll create a power vacuum where the person will start striving for your validation, and this is the crux of most negative relationships.

When you don't genuinely validate your partner, but you're allowing them to open up, they end up trying harder to get your validation. Over many weeks, months, or even years, this can create such an unbalanced power dynamic. The needy partner is constantly harassing the partner for attention and acceptance or will shut down completely, perhaps opening up to other people outside the relationship, which risks a whole new set of problems.

For some people, they may get a kick out of someone constantly craving validation from them. It's a temporary fix that someone wants them and their connectivity so badly, but again, long term, there are no winners. Whenever you create a power imbalance in a relationship, you have a "winner" and a "loser," but the winner has to live with the loser, making both people losers. The real winning comes from genuinely caring about each other and wanting to support each other's growth, healing, and development.

Sure, there are going to be times when you have a stressful day, you're tired, you're sick, or you're dealing with a load of other things, and your partner wants to open up to you. This is the make-or-break moment where you either genuinely tell them that you can talk about it later, or you move forward disingenuously. It can be a hard decision to make, especially if you want to be there for your partner, but if you need a rest first, then say, "Can we talk about this a bit later? Perhaps this evening, where I'll be able to give you my full attention?"

This is much more respectful than just going forward with the conversation, going through the motions, not giving your partner your full attention, and then having to deal with all the negative consequences that come from that approach.

To summarize:

- Be genuine in your conversations and interactions
- If you're not interested, tell the other person respectfully
- If you want to support someone but need to take care of yourself first, let the other person know respectfully

And with that, we come to the end of this chapter.

Agreeably, that was a bit of a chunky chapter with a lot to take in, but that is the main component of proper listening, and mastering these steps will take you so incredibly far. As I said above, like any skill, it will take practice to wrap your head around, but you'll get there.

Just take the process one step at a time, taking small steps by applying a bit of the technique here and there, and you'll see such big progress as time moves on.

However, we're not done yet. There are still plenty of listening concepts we need to cover, like overcoming the common and not-so-common obstacles you may come across when conversing with different people and, most importantly, how to see if people are actually saying what they want to say and are telling you an honest message, which is exactly what I'm going to be talking about in the next chapter.

Chapter Five - The Art of Mindreading Through Awareness

"It is understanding that gives us an ability to have peace. When we understand the other fellow's viewpoint, and he understands ours, then we can sit down and work out our differences." Harry S. Truman

There have been countless times in my life where I'm speaking to someone, and I'm hearing what they're saying. However, the message of the actual words they're using doesn't make any sense in the conversation context.

In the light of our global listening problem, it should go without saying that misunderstanding is a huge part of the problem. We live in a world of emojis, texting, and digital messaging, and we've become lazy with how we speak to one another.

I'm sure you've had a text, and you've been unsure of whether the person who sent it is happy, sad, sarcastic, passive-aggressive, or a mixture of all of them, which only leaves you scratching your head, unsure of the best way to respond. Whether you're talking online or face-to-face, a massive part of listening is having the skills to decipher what someone is saying and tunneling your way down to the true message they're trying to give you.

Let's start with the basics. Say someone comes up to you and says something along the lines of:

> "I really loved our date tonight. It was perfect."

I know. It sounds simple, but there's very little room here to misinterpret what someone is saying. Every word here conveys positive emotions and makes you feel good about what's being said. Easy peasy. Try this one:

> "My god. It was absolutely brutal!"

Again, going off words alone, you imagine something like a breakup or a fight has just happened, and someone's ended up getting really hurt. It was "brutal." This implies negative connotations, but, what happens if someone is actually talking about the horror movie they've just seen, and when they say it was brutal, this is actually a really positive thing?

As you can see, the first step in understanding what someone is saying is to understand the context of what they're talking about.

Take a moment to think about what someone is saying and the topic they are on, and it will give you a much greater understanding of what is being said. This goes back to what we were saying about being present in your conversations.

Even if you zone out for a sentence or two, you can completely lose what is going on. This is guaranteed to make the person feel as though they're not being listened to.

Of course, this is all basic stuff. Understand the context of a conversation, and you'll be able to understand the message that's being told to you. Still, humans and the way they converse with each other are typically more complicated than the simple examples above. The act of "mindreading" someone to find out the deeper messages also goes a lot deeper than this.

Learning to Engage with Your Gut Instinct

I've teased this point throughout this book, and that's because gut instinct is such a massive part of human psychology. It can teach you so much as long as you're willing to tune in and listen to it. Your brain is an amazing thing in this way if you can put it to good use.

The chances are you've been with someone, and they've said that everything is fine, but you have that deep-rooted inner feeling that it's really not. Perhaps you've got home from work, and your partner is aggressively tidying the house.

"Hey, is everything okay? You seem stressed."

"Yup. Everything is fine."

"Are you sure? You can talk to me."

"Yup."

As your partner darts about the room cleaning up, they're not making eye contact with you, they're speaking in short, abrupt sentences, and not engaging with you in the way they normally do. Going off verbal cues alone, perhaps if these sentences were sent over text messages, you would feel you're right in thinking everything is okay, but in reality, this doesn't seem to be the case.

There are so many factors here that your body is picking up on and your mind is processing. Their lack of engagement, eye contact, and connectedness with you. Their tone of voice. Their bluntness. You're a human being who has been around for decades. You've got a memory bank full of experiences that gives your brain enough information to know when someone who says they're okay really isn't. Your natural, intuitive mind is programmed to recognize these signs, also known as your gut instinct.

The concept of "gut instinct" has been around for a very long time and is a very well-researched area of human behavior and psychology.

Psychologist Daniel Kahneman, who was awarded the Nobel Memorial Prize back in 2002, called this bodily function "System 1." Gary Klein, Ph.D., the author of *Sources of Power,* talks about how emergency services staff, such as firefighters and medical staff, rely on gut instincts to make literal life-or-death decisions, based on the information their brains can process in a matter of seconds, without having to step back and overthink and analyze a situation.

Malcolm Gladwell, the Canadian author, journalist, and public speaker, wrote *Blink,* a book where he talks about how our gut instinct is always active and always working. He uses examples like how our brain can press the brakes on our cars while traveling at high speeds on a highway when approaching stand-still traffic or grabbing your young child if they look like they're going to fall off the sofa.

You've probably experienced gut instinct in full effect yourself when you feel as though you're going to drop your phone, and you instantly do a little dance with your arms to stop it from falling to the ground. You didn't think about doing that action. Your brain just does it.

I could go on and on about all the advocates for the power of instinct, but I'm sure you get the idea. Bringing it back to conversations, your brain uses these gut instinct systems to judge the experience you're having when talking to someone else. If you get an impulse that someone is feeling a certain way or something isn't quite right, the chances are the impulse is correct.

But, not all the time. Yeah, I'm going to make things confusing now.

If human beings solely relied on gut instinct decisions, our relationships would fail. Our businesses would crumble because gut instinct is all about living in the moment and making decisions that benefit us now, rather than planning for the long term. The decision-making process doesn't take into account things like logic and analytical behaviors.

The takeaway here is to use your gut instinct in conversations as a first step to gauge how someone is feeling and what kind of message they're giving you. Noticing this impulse message, you can then bring in your analytical brain to make logical decisions on how you're going to proceed in your conversation.

Let's go back to the first example with your partner frantically cleaning up and see how it plays out.

> "Hey, is everything okay? You seem stressed."

> "Yup. Everything is fine."

Your gut instinct is triggered. You know from your partner's body language and tone of voice that your partner isn't fine. Your gut instinct has done part of its job. Now bring in your analytical thinking mind. What's the best way to respond? Here are some options.

- "Yeah, everything is fine? Are you sure about that?"

- "I can tell something is wrong. Talk to me."

- Just accept they are feeling okay and take what they're saying as the truth.

- "You don't seem okay. If you want to talk about it, I'm here."

- "Well, okay then."

- "Hey. Come here. Talk to me. What's up?"

There are multiple approaches here that could lead to positive and negative outcomes. You might say, "Well, okay then," and that just upsets your partner even more because they were unconsciously testing whether you cared enough to talk about what was wrong with them. The last option is probably the best for most situations because it shows you're stopping what you're doing and putting them at the center of the conversation. It shows you're ready to provide support.

However, the best approach for you will depend on the person you're speaking to and the relationship you have with them. In other words, use your logical, thinking mind to consider the person you're speaking with and their past behaviors, and how they are currently in effect.

If your partner is the type of person to say that everything is okay when it's not, and this has been a common past experience, then you know there's a high chance something is wrong, but perhaps they don't want to burden you with their problems. In a situation like this, using everything you know, you can validate how your partner feels, say it's okay to talk about their problems, and they can vent if they want to, and then the conversation can proceed.

Using psychology skills, you've just listened to the real meaning behind what someone is saying and moved the conversation on in the best possible way.

Considerations and Thinks to Look Out For

While these figures can vary depending on individuals, cultures, and prior conditioning, most communication can be broken down into:

- 55% body language
- 38% tone of voice
- 7% verbal words and chosen language

When you really want to listen to what someone is saying, you're going to need to look at their body language first, then their tone of voice, then the words they're saying, and this way, you'll get a very accurate idea of the message someone is giving you. So, let's start at the top.

How to Read Body Language

This section will be a bit of a crash course where I'll show you the basics of reading body language, which will be more than enough to help you read the vast majority of people you meet and interact with within your day-to-day life. However, bear in mind this isn't the complete guide. If you want to know more as you're developing your skills, there are plenty of books and courses out there dedicated to the art of body language and explaining the nuances of this skill.

Start with the eyes

Many believe the eyes are the gateway to the soul, which is true when it comes to the truth of a conversation. If someone has a real lack of eye contact, it means they could be trying to avoid the truth and can't look you in the eyes because they know what they're saying isn't true, or they're ashamed of something. They could also be nervous or intimidated, which makes them not want to make eye contact.

Think about children who will instinctively look down at the ground when they're embarrassed or are getting told off after they've been caught doing something red-handed. The same applies to adults. Likewise, however, if someone is making too much eye contact, this could be a sign that they're forcing eye contact, or it could mean anger and hate. Think about times you've been so angry with someone, and you're just trying to stare them down.

Alternatively, there are positive emotions linked with intense eye contact, such as affection, longing, flirting, interest, and desire. This means you need to judge the context of the conversation (as we discussed earlier) since this will also affect the message you're receiving.

Ideally, in any situation, you want a balanced amount of eye contact that lasts a few seconds, then you can look away, perhaps to think, and then go back to making eye contact. This indicates an honest and forthcoming person.

Recognize posture

Someone's posture is a massive indication of how they're feeling and what message they are sending. If someone is sitting or standing with a straight, upright back, with their head held high, this means they are comfortable and confident in the situation, but it can also portray feelings of authority and power. Either way, a confident posture indicates they are engaged in the conversation.

On the other hand, someone who is depressed, sad, or intimidated will shrink away. On a physical level, this is someone's physical attempt to make themselves smaller as though hiding from the interaction and making themselves less noticeable. Hunched or raised shoulders also indicate stress.

If someone has their arms and hands open with their chest exposed, this is a very vulnerable position to be in and usually means they trust you. Any kind of body language that exposes the chest means this because, in the wild and before civilized times, having an exposed chest meant something would be able to hurt you quite easily.

On the flip side, if someone is closed off, has their arms crossed in front of their chest, or covers parts of themselves more than usual, this is a sign they are uncomfortable, anxious, or defensive.

Handshakes or hugs

Whenever someone shakes your hand, the level of grip you feel indicates how the other person is feeling within the situation. A firm or intensely firm handshake is a sign of confidence and power, but a weak handshake is a sign of nervousness and shyness. An overly strong handshake can be taken as a sign of aggression.

Watch their smile

It's very easy for someone to fake a smile to hide when they're feeling negative or trying to hide their emotions. We all know the classic fake smile actors do in movies when they've gone through a breakup or lost their job, and they're trying to let everyone know they're feeling okay.

However, while smiles can be faked, you can easily see the giveaways if you're paying attention. If someone is giving you a real, genuine smile, you will see a crinkle appear in the corner of both of their eyes, creating what is typically referred to as "crow's feet." See this pattern during a smile, and you know the person is genuinely comfortable and happy in this situation.

Note physical proximity

While a traditional body language trait, it will be interesting to see what happens now we're hopefully coming to the end of the COVID-19 pandemic. With social distancing happening for over a year now, many people will find it strange to be standing close to others, especially if they're strangers or people at work.

That being said, physical proximity is a massive part of non-verbal communication. Simply put, if someone is standing or sitting close to you, this means they're comfortable in your personal space and enjoy having you close. If someone is standing a distance apart from you, then they are keeping a distance between you to feel safe.

A note on the tone of voice and inflection

A very important part of reading someone, the tone of voice and inflection someone is using makes up, on average, around 38% of their total communication, which shows it's such a huge consideration to think about. Fortunately, it's relatively easy to judge the tone of voice of someone. You just need to keep an ear open for the volume they're talking at and the kind of tone they have.

This sounds like simple stuff. If someone is shouting at you and sounds irritated, the chances are that they're angry and irritated. You might be reading this like, *Well, dur. Obviously!* but there's a fair few people in my own life that don't seem to grasp this simple concept.

A woman I used to work with used to never get a hint that she talked way too much. During lunch breaks, we'd go into the city to get something to eat, and she would talk about everything that's going on in her life. It was fine. It wasn't horrible or anything like that, but everyone would let her get on with it. But as time went on, people would reply with less enthusiasm and would make it very clear with their tones of voice that they were bored.

"Yes, Hannah. Cool." (Read in the most boring voice you can muster.) But still, she never got the hint because she was never listening to what others had to say. My mother was the same. She would get so stuck trying to prove her point when arguing with my father that she never seemed to notice his tone of voice change from diplomatic to annoyed.

In short, keep an ear open for the tone of voice someone is using since it will tell you so much.

And finally, I want to talk about inflection. Inflection is the term given to emphasis placed on certain words that completely change the meaning of the sentence. Take a look at the following sentences and see if you can figure out the meanings behind them.

Statement

> "I didn't tell him you took the last piece of cake."

Any ideas? The words are the same, but how the sentence is said completely redefines the message behind it.

Statement	Meaning
"I didn't tell him you took the last piece of cake."	"I told someone, but not him, that you took the piece of cake."
"I didn't tell him you took the last piece of cake."	"I told him you took something else instead of the piece of cake."
"I didn't tell him you took the last piece of cake."	"I didn't tell him you took the piece of cake."
"I didn't tell him you took the last piece of cake."	"I'm lying that I didn't tell him you took the piece of cake."

It's essential for effective communication that you take the time to listen to the nuances of how things are said to you because it can mean so much.

A lot of the skill for doing this ties back in with what we said earlier about going with your gut instinct because it's this part of you that will notice it first. If you feel the impulse of your gut, take a note of what's been said and how it makes you feel, then replay what's been said to get to the true meaning.

Summary on Body Language

Reading all of these cues can take skill and practice, but it's so interesting once you start noticing the traits because the vast majority of people will follow these rules unconsciously and without thinking. Speaking unconsciously without any control or mindfulness is basically a habit for most people, meaning it's a great way to read the situation and what people say to you.

Combining everything you've learned already, if someone is really personal and open, but they're keeping their distance from you and have their arms crossed, while their words say they're comfortable, their body language suggests otherwise.

Using this information, you can then decide whether the person is being genuine to you or identify what their motives could be.

How to Tell When Someone is Lying

There's a big difference between someone saying they're okay when they're not because they don't want to burden you with their troubles or don't have the energy to go into what they're going through—and someone flat-out, maliciously lying to you, or perhaps even gaslighting you.

The truth is that everybody lies. In an interview with British QC, Jordan Peterson stated that "Everybody lies, but the trick is to be incredibly careful about how you do it, to whom, and your motives behind masking the truth."

Put it this way. If you're lying about stealing something from someone and you're claiming someone else did it, even though it was you, that makes you a fairly malicious person. However, if you're lying to someone because you're taking them to their surprise birthday party, this is one of the more acceptable lies.

That being said, modern-day humans seem to lie far more often than you may believe.

According to 2017 statistics, 90% of children will have grasped the concept of lying by the age of four, and some estimates suggest that around 60% of adults can't talk for more than ten minutes without lying or distorting the truth more than once. The average was lying three times within that time frame.

Here are some other "fun" statistics:

- 12% of adults lie often

- 13% of patients will lie to their doctors

- 30% of adults lie about their diet and exercise habits

- Women lie three times a day to their partners, coworkers, and bosses

- Men tell six lies a day to the same people

- Lying is more common in phone calls than face-to-face conversation

- 10% of lies are exaggerations

- 60% are blatant deceptions of the truth

As you can see, averaging speaking, lying is quite commonplace (unless people lied in the surveys!), and having the ability to see through these lies to get the truth out of people, or being able to confirm when someone is directly telling you the truth, can be an incredibly useful skill to have.

Whether you lie (even if it's now and then) or your coworkers and partners are lying to you, it's something you need to be aware of. Truth and honesty are the best foundations possible for any kind of relationship. These statistics on how often people lie clearly indicate why so many modern relationships fail.

Estimates suggest over 50% of relationships will fail. The main reasons why from couples surveyed?? This is the order from Darcy Sterling, Ph.D. writing for *Psychology Today*:

- Trust issues
- Communication issues
- Different life priorities
- Different values
- And so on

Notice how the two first items she lists are trust issues and communication issues? If you can sort out the quality of communication in your relationship and base your connection on trust and honesty, your relationships will improve infinitely.

So, how do you do it? How do you figure out when someone is lying to you? The best way is to keep an eye open for the signs.

The Signs of Lying

These are signs of lying inspired from Pamela Meyer's *Liespotting* book, as well as her sixteen-million-view TED Talk (which is available on YouTube by searching her name), and are the key signs you'll want to look out for in your conversations.

Inconsistency in the message

The majority of people will lie off the cuff because they're hiding a certain fact, don't want to own up to something, or don't want to admit the truth, and are making up a story to cover themselves and something they've done.

However, people put way less thought into these lies than you would first believe, meaning it's very easy to catch people out when you ask them to repeat the details.

This is known as "'getting your story straight."

If you ask someone who's telling the truth to repeat their story, the details will always remain the same. Stories that are actually lies tend to change every retelling, which is why this is deemed the most consistent way to catch someone lying to you. Here's how you can implement this technique to find out.

"And then the dog ran out into the road and was nearly hit by this truck. It was so scary!"

"The dog nearly got hit? Wow. How fast was the motorbike going?"

"Pretty fast."

In this example, you weren't corrected by intentionally repeating with an incorrect detail, which can be seen as a tell-tale sign the person is lying. Sometimes, you won't notice someone is lying because they'll tell you a story, and you won't recognize the change in details until you hear it again, which could be weeks or months later. Again, if your gut instinct picks up on something, then the chances are you've just cottoned onto a lie.

Body language and expressions

We spoke a lot about body language in the last section, so I'll make this quick. There are some tell-tale expressions and physical signs someone is lying, and if you spot them, then it may be time to pay closer attention to what is being said so you're able to find out the truth.

Some of these psychological signs that typically happen unconsciously include things like:

- Fake smiles

- Rapid blinking

- Flaring nostrils

- Excessive hand movements. A study back in 2015 carried out by the University of Michigan found that people who lie use their hands far more in conversation than those who tell the truth.

- Fidgeting or Itching. If someone is lying, they will typically be restless, pick at their nails, or play with their hair, and try to fidget around as though trying to get comfortable.

- A lack of eye contact. People who are lying tend to avoid making eye contact with you.

- Lip movements. If someone is rolling their lips or can't keep them still, this can be a sign they are lying to you. It's as though the body is unconsciously trying to hold back the truth.

The important thing to remember here is that these aren't confirmations that someone is lying, but more subconscious indications that they could be. If you notice them, focus harder on what is being said to make your own decision, mixing this sign with the others on this list.

Stalling in conversation

If you're calling someone up on a lie or asking for more detail on a story, you may notice a pause in the conversation that could be the other person stalling for time as they think of an answer, especially if they've been asked a very unexpected question.

A: "Yeah, I can't believe how amazing it was that I bumped into Michael Jackson in New York. I was so starstruck!"

B: "Sounds amazing. What's he like in person?"

A: "Just like you would expect. Quiet. A bit reserved. I can't believe nobody else around us noticed him."

B: "Whereabouts did you see him?"

A: "Oh, what? Where did I see him? Like where in New York?"

B: "Yeah."

A: "Oh, just in Times Square. Not sure where exactly. Just out on the street."

Again, repeating the question is not a confirmation that someone is lying, but if this sign appears alongside other points we've spoken about, and it happens frequently, then the chances are that you could be being fed lies.

A suddenness to stop or move on the conversation

Another important sign you should look out for is someone telling you something and then wanting to drastically change the conversation. If someone is abruptly hurrying a conversation onto a new subject out of the blue, is trying to take the focus off of themselves, and ultimately doesn't want to hang around on the point they've just made, then it could have been a lie.

A: "Yeah, I can't believe I won $10 on a scratch-off. It's the first time I've won anything."

B: "I won $100 on a scratch-off once."

A: "Oh, cool. What did you spend it on?"

B: "Oh. Not much. Which card did you buy?"

A: "Just the $2 one. Come on, $100? You must have been so happy."

B: "Yeah. Wasn't bad. Hey, listen. What are you doing for the rest of the day?"

A: "Probably going to treat myself to a nice lunch. What about you?"

And so on. You can imagine the readiness to move on in conversation if A was lying about their win because they had nothing really to add to the conversation, nor was being very happy for B.

The choice of language

While not a tell-tale way to prove someone is lying, the language someone chooses to use can be another indication when paired with the other points in this section. If someone has to remind you or convince you they're not lying, they will use language to help their cause. You may hear statements like:

- Honestly, it did happen.

- I swear on so-and-so's life.

- I swear on the Bible that...

- If I'm being completely honest...

And so on. Other signs here can include someone giving you way too much detail in a story. It's as though they're trying to make the story as believable as possible or going back on what they've already said to change the details they've told you in an attempt to make it more realistic.

As with most of these points, don't notice just one and convince yourself the person is lying. Instead, if you notice a sign, look for the other signs and then piece what they are saying together. If it happens frequently and lots of signs are met, then the person could be lying.

Identifying a lie allows you to choose how you proceed. You can call them up on it, let it slide, or be extra mindful of seeing if they lie anymore. Whatever approach you take is up to you and depends on what you want out of the relationship you're referring to.

Understanding the Power of Motives

Every human being in the world is motivated by something. Every single decision you make is a motivation in action, whether you're aware that you're doing it or not. On a basic level, you eat because you're motivated by hunger, and drink because you're motivated by thirst. Your body motivates you to do these things because otherwise, well, you'll die.

Things can get a little more complicated when it comes to your goals, relationships, and day-to-day habits. You might be dieting, motivated by an Instagram post you saw, or a pair of jeans you want to fit into by the time summer comes around. But you might eat a huge bit of cake because you're motivated to feel better after a bad day. Our motivations overlap all the time. Our priorities are constantly changing depending on what's happening in our lives.

When it comes to conversations, it's important to think about what people are motivated by when they're talking to you, so you're able to find out the truth of what they're saying and whether there are any hidden agendas you need to be aware of.

You can get all this from listening and taking time to understand what's being said to you, but mindfully highlighting someone's motive can really open up the truth about the situation you're in. Take this conversation as an example.

A: "Hey. Do you mind going to get me a coffee?"

B: "Er, sure. I'll do it after I've booked the meeting room. Just waiting for the computer."

A: "Ah, I would really appreciate having one now. I need to go to see a client soon."

B: "Okay. Be right back."

What's happening here? You may think it's a conversation happening between a businessman and their assistant, and he needs his coffee before his meeting. If this is the case, then he may really need some help because he's so busy.

However, depending on the context of the situation, it could be two employees talking, and both want to book the meeting room, and person A is trying to get person B to get a coffee, so he gets the first pick of the available meeting room slots.

This kind of thing is what we call a "hidden agenda," and to be the best listener possible, you need to know how you can identify when someone is genuine with you and when someone is trying to get something out of you (or someone else you're close to) without you realizing.

Fortunately, the psychology of human behavior and communication research has the answers to help you dive deeper and highlight the truth in what someone is up to and is trying to manipulate you with their own secret missions.

The conversation is always about them

If someone is trying to manipulate you, then the chances are they will always have the subject of conversation revolve around them. However, while in the conversation, this can be very difficult to notice. This is why you must be able to take a step back and see the reality of a situation.

Again, a lot of this is going to rely on your gut instinct.

This is typical behavior from people with hidden agendas since they are typically narcissistic people who are out to get what they want. This can't happen if people aren't talking about them and their wants or desires. If there's an impatience around someone and they want to get back to talking about them, then make sure you pay special attention to this conversation trend.

You are continually talking about a certain subject

Hand in hand with the consideration above, if someone has a hidden agenda, you may not notice at first. Still, if the person you're speaking with keeps coming back to the same subject over and over again, then this can be a clear sign that they haven't yet received the outcome they want and are once again trying to force it.

The standard lack of body language

Just like when people are lying to you, if someone is trying to force a narrative or has a secret agenda they're trying to push through, the body physically matches this deception with the classic tell-tale signs like a lack of eye contact or stiffness of the body.

If someone is a true narcissist, they may have picked up on this trait and learned how to force body language to make themselves more believable. However, since you also know the tricks of the trade, you'll easily be able to tell the difference between someone genuinely being themselves and someone who's being fake.

They explore different approaches with the same goal

Another approach that couples with the signs I've mentioned above is someone trying to force the same outcome, but they're using different conversational approaches, usually within the same conversation. While they may not directly be suggesting something, they are trying to get the outcome they want through force.

For example, let's say someone is manipulating their group of friends to go to a Chinese-styled takeaway while everyone is deciding where to go out for food. Perhaps a relatively harmless example, but the same principles can apply in any conversation.

They may say things like:

- Why don't we go to Golden House?

- Last time we went to Golden House, you said you really liked it.

- It's a really nice atmosphere there.

- Didn't you go there for a birthday a few years ago? What did you think?

- Well, if you guys can't decide, we should just go to Golden House.

- You don't want to walk far? It's only two blocks away.

They show manipulative tendencies

This point may seem a little obvious, but if you're not on the lookout for it nor aware that someone has manipulative tendencies, then it's easy to forget yourself and just take what they're saying at face value.

If someone has proven to be a manipulative person in the past, whether they have acted that way directly to you, or you know they have acted that way to other people, always take what they're saying with a pinch of salt and keep your eyes open for hidden agendas.

You feel used

Again, this is your gut instinct being the very powerful force of nature that it is. If you've just finished interacting with someone and you *feel,* deep down, like you're being used and manipulated, then take a step back and evaluate the situation. Why do you feel that way? What was it that the person you said or did that made you feel used?

Perhaps the answer is obvious, or maybe you can't put your finger on it. The most important thing is that you become aware of the feeling itself and apply caution when heading into any future interactions with that person.

How to Deal With Gaslighting

The final point I want to discuss within this chapter is the act of gaslighting.

Gaslighting has been a massive talking point over the last few years, a term made popular back in 1944 in the movie *Gaslight*. *Gaslight* was a movie about a young couple where the man manipulated his wife into thinking she was crazy by distorting her reality. Over time, this made her doubt whether she was sane, ultimately not being able to trust herself and putting all her will and control into the hands of her husband, who basically dictated her life.

The movie got the name from the fact he would dim the gaslight lamps in the room whenever she was out. Whenever she returned to the room, she would question that the room became darker, to which he would deny that ever happened. When this happens all the time, the wife began to doubt her thoughts, leading to her thinking she was crazy.

This kind of manipulation and hidden agenda happens so often in modern-day society that it's actually crazy.

There are stories of it happening in the media all the time, especially with the rise of movements like #MeToo. Domestic abuse cases at home are still so high—about 20% of children in UK households live with some degree of domestic violence—there's no doubt that gaslighting is happening since it's a core part of victim control.

So, what can you do about it, and how can you use listening to know whether you're being gaslighted? First, you need to start listening to what's being said to you.

Have you ever shared a point of view, only for it to be shot down?

In a bleak example, let's say you saw a message from a coworker pop up on your partner's phone.

You only catch the preview, but it looks pretty flirty. You're a bit concerned and bring it up to your partner, who dismisses you and says the text doesn't exist. You're sure it did. After all, you saw it with your own eyes, but your partner saying it doesn't make you doubt that you ever saw it all. Thus, you've been gaslit and made to doubt yourself and your sanity. This is a dangerous path to be on.

Some really easy statements to look out for that can gaslight you include lines like:

- It was only a joke. Don't be so sensitive.

- You're crazy. That's not how things happened at all.

- Do you really think you know what you're talking about?

- You're definitely imagining that.

Now, just because you may have heard these statements before, that doesn't mean you're definitely being gaslighted.

Let's say your partner says that they are happy to go and visit your parents over the weekend in two weeks. Then the two weeks come around, and they say something like:

"No, you definitely said we're visiting your parents next week, not this week. I have a lot of work I have to do this weekend and can't go."

Maybe gaslighting, but it could be an honest mistake from either side. Perhaps you did say three weeks instead of two, or perhaps your partner misheard you (this is why it's so important to practice effective communication in your relationships because then situations like this will never happen!), and that's fine.

However, if you're experiencing situations like this repeatedly, then gaslighting is certainly something you're going to want to be aware of and on the lookout for. Some of the key ways you can be gaslighted include techniques like:

Countering You	If something happens, the gaslighter may switch around the event, so you are in the wrong, even if you're not. They may fabricate new details of the event or deny certain things have happened.
Trivializing What You Say	Whatever feelings you share, they invalidate quickly. They say that how you feel and your emotions don't matter. They may also suggest that you're overreacting.
Withholding Information	Whenever you try to discuss a situation, they dismiss your arguments. They may claim that you're trying to confuse them with what you're saying.
Forgetting or Denying	If you share details of an event, they may completely forget or deny

Statements and Events	that certain things have or haven't happened to prove their point.
Discrediting Your Thoughts	Will state that you're unable to recall details properly will give examples of the past (true or not) where you proved what you say can't be trusted, thus invalidating what you're saying now.
Diverting Your Conversations	If you bring a conversation up and it's quickly dismissed as though it's not important, and the conversation is forced to be moved on without you being listened to.

If you're noticing traits like these on a regular and consistent basis, then it's time to start thinking about what you can do to stop yourself from being gaslighted.

Remember, you may be gaslighted by your partner, coworkers, boss, customers, and so on. It isn't just restricted to your personal life.

The Five Steps to Identifying and Dealing with Gaslighting

Step One - Identify the Gaslighting

We've covered this in the previous section, so I'll be quick. Suppose you notice any of the signs we spoke about above. In that case, you feel regularly invalidated in your conversations, you doubt yourself, constantly ask yourself whether you're too much of a sensitive person, frequently apologize for your actions or sharing your thoughts, and generally feel unhappy when around a certain person, then you could be being gaslighted.

Step Two - Step Back

As you can tell from Step One, if you're being gaslighted, then there will be many confusing and contrasting emotions spinning around in your head. Although you've practiced emotional intelligence to deal with this, it can be a good idea to step back and take a breather from the situation.

It's always important to remain calm in any given situation. Otherwise, you're not going to have the best outcomes when you address the issues. Practice taking a time out, whether that means going for a walk, meditating, reading, or however you're able to take a break.

Step Three - Build Your Case

Next, you need evidence to secure your side of the story. You may want to start doing things like screenshotting emails and text messages, noting the times and dates of conversations you're having, and even writing down quotes from conversations.

With this solid proof that you're recording after a conversation has taken place, then you know your version of events is real. If the person you're involved with denies that something happened, then you know with absolute certainty that you're being gaslighted.

Step Four - Address the Behavior

Once you're certain you're being gaslighted, it's time to speak up. In the best-case scenario, the person you address will realize what they're doing and vow to be better. In which case, you can watch the journey and move forward. If the behavior comes back, you'll need to start again.

However, if you're dealing with a true narcissist, then they may agree to defuse the situation, or they may dismiss what you're saying completely. For example, a coworker may say something like, "You've done no work this week and definitely aren't pulling your weight."

You can then address the behavior by saying, "That isn't true. I've completed these tasks for the week. Would you like to go through them with me now?" This is where your evidence comes in. Remember, when addressing this behavior, remain calm, neutral, and polite.

Step Five - Moving Forward

Depending on the last few steps' outcomes, you've got some decisions to make on how you want to move forward. If the person denies that anything wrong is happening, it could be time to get other people involved. If they are your partner, you may want to go to counseling.

If they don't want help or still deny anything is wrong, then you may want to start thinking about leaving the relationship and moving on. This can be a hard decision to make, but if you're unhappy with your life, then going into a new chapter is certainly going to be better for you in the long run.

The most important thing to remember throughout this process is to focus on yourself and your own self-care. It's important to keep an eye on how you're looking after yourself, your habits, and your levels of peace. This could sound a little spiritual, but you'll be amazed at how much more capable you'll be at dealing with the situation when you're at peak physical and mental health.

As you can see, there's a lot of power that comes with listening, especially when it comes to more complicated relationships like one when someone in your life is gaslighting you. If you're worried about being gaslighted and you want more information, then there's a ton of advice out there that can help you with your own personal journey. Remember, you never have to go through that process alone.

There are always support networks out there for you to help you move away from toxic relationships and to deal with the effects of gaslighting.

Phew. That was a chunky chapter, but one that's so important when you're trying to understand other people and use your listening skills to develop the best, most satisfying relationship possible with the right people in your life.

As we come to the end of this book, we have but two chapters to go. Next, we'll discuss some of the potential problems you may encounter while listening to other people, basically highlighting things to look out for to make your skills even better. Then we'll talk about how you can do everything you've learned to become the best conversationalist you can be.

Let's go!

Chapter Six - Addressing the Obstacles of Listening

"No one is as deaf as the man who will not listen." Proverb

This chapter is going to be short and sweet. We've spoken a lot about some of the potential problems you'll encounter when trying to listen to someone else. As a quick recap, these tips included things like:

- Minimizing distractions
- Removing conversational expectations
- Not judging the other person
- Acknowledging your biases towards people or conversation subjects

And so on. Check back to chapter three if you need to refresh your memory. However, these aren't the only barriers you may come across, so this is what we're going to dive into here in a quick-fire guide that will clear up any loose ends that are left to clear up.

Avoid Having Multiple Conversations at Once

Perhaps a no-brainer to some, but it's easy to get caught into the trap of having multiple conversations at once, whether that means literally having conversations with the people around you or listening to talks on the TV or radio.

I remember working in my last firm and having the annual Christmas meal. Three conversations were going on around me: one on each side of me and the other on the opposite side of the table. It was so hard to focus or give my attention to any of them.

Instead, pick a conversation and stick to it, politely declining other conversational opportunities until you're ready to move on.

Not Making Judgments Based on Physical Appearance

Just because you don't find the person you're speaking with physically attractive or sexy doesn't mean you can't listen to what they have to say.

Likewise, if you find the person attractive, you may be distracted by their looks and not listening to what they say. Pay attention to your thoughts, acknowledge your wandering mind, and gently bring your focus back to the conversation at hand. This is another reason why it pays to be mindful.

Not Being Interested

Granted, you're not going to find every single conversation you have the most exciting conversation in the world, and there are topics you simply won't be interested in.

However, instead of just letting the other person talk and you end up drifting away, you can literally just say, "I'm not interested in this kind of conversation," or "I'm just not as passionate about this subject as you." Here's an example where you won't come across as being rude nor risk offending the person you're talking to. It depends on how much confidence you can say it with.

A: "So I got these new fish, and one is a Korean Koi, and I have to keep the outdoor pond heated to 60 degrees, but then I got this isolation tube to put in the end to stop it losing temperature as it goes through the filter."

B: "Ah, I'm sorry. I'm naive about this kind of thing. I'm glad you're so passionate about it, though. It's nice to see that people are still passionate about things these days."

A: "Oh yes. I'm very passionate. I love my fish."

B: "That's really nice. I can see it in your eyes you mean it as well. Anyway, I must bounce. My lunch break is over. Catch up soon?"

As long as you're saying these statements in a calm, polite, and friendly way, there shouldn't be a problem. I know we spoke about not interrupting someone earlier, and we just did in this situation, but you're not doing it in a rude way where you're trying to force your point of view down someone's throat.

Instead, you're not interested in the conversation, and you're still able to break free from it in a way that isn't offensive. If you remain in the conversation and get bored, you're much more likely to leave in an abusive way. Of course, you'll have emotional intelligence training to stop that from happening, but some people can really test you from time to time.

Not Empathizing with the Other Person

We've touched on this briefly, but empathizing with someone is not the same as sympathizing with them. To have sympathy is to pity the person you're speaking with for their situation, but to have empathy is to proactively put yourself in their shoes to feel and understand how they're feeling.

Both ways of connecting to the other person will help you listen in different ways because you'll be able to feel the emotions of the speaker, therefore having more insight into the message behind what they're saying. For example:

A: "I just don't know what to do with my relationship. I love him a lot, but there's so many little things I can't stand about him. I don't know if I'm just kidding myself."

B: "I get that it's hard when you have so many feelings. How long have you been together?"

A: "About six years now."

B: "That's a long time with someone. It's no wonder it's hard. Anybody would feel the same. Have you spoken to him about how you feel?"

Notice in this example how there are plenty of opportunities to put yourself in the shoes of person A. You can imagine how hard it can be to be in a relationship for so long but not be happy. Become the person you're speaking with and really try to show as much compassion as you can.

For clarity, it would be incredibly unempathetic and soulless to say things like:

- Just dump him and move.

- Oh, just be grateful you're in a relationship

- There are plenty more fish in the sea

- Just fight it out with him

Being Affected by Physical or Mental Health

If you're not feeling well, you're sick, hungry, thirsty, tired, exhausted, or mentally drained, then these are all reasons why you may not be capable of listening to someone properly. It's okay to feel like this, and if you feel like it's affecting your ability to listen, then you can politely say to the person talking that you're not feeling as though you're giving them the attention they deserve, and you would be happy to carry on this conversation at a later date.

And there we have it, some of the key barriers you'll come up against in your journey to becoming a better listener. By combining everything from all the chapters in this book, you'll be able to rapidly become an incredible listener who can take on board new ideas, connect and empathize with other people, and have all the required foundations for building the most meaningful relationships with the people in your life.

Of course, there is one more stop on your journey, which is to now, after listening to the other person talk, to respond in a productive and meaningful way. Our last chapter is all about continuing the conversation.

147

Chapter Seven - Continuing the Conversation

"Conversation should touch everything, but should concentrate itself on nothing." Oscar Wilde

First, you may be thinking, *Hey, we already covered validation, so surely that's what I'll say next and how I respond?* and you'd be right. However, this chapter is all about sharing a few points to help you focus on the conversation at hand and give you a solid foundation to generate a response to anything you've been told that will help you effectively convey your ideas, thoughts, feelings, and emotions.

There's no time to mess around now!

How to Respond in a Conversation

Let's start with an example. Your boss comes into your office, and he's not happy. He's stressed. The project you and the team are working on doesn't look like it's going to be done by the deadline, and the client is not going to be happy. He comes over to you to try and get things moving and says something along the lines of:

"Right, this isn't looking good. The deadline for the project is on Friday, and we're nowhere close. We're over budget and so behind. What can we do?"

How do you respond?

Taking from everything we've learned, you'll go through the following process.

First, don't take what is being said personally. Your boss is talking to you but not blaming you for the problem, even if they say something that makes it feel that way. If you do feel that way, notice the emotion and don't take it personally.

Using empathy, put yourself in your boss's shoes and notice that they are probably taking heat from both the customer and their bosses, and now they're trying to get the situation resolved. So, your boss is stressed, under pressure, and looking for answers. Let's start with validating their feelings with something like:

Understandably, everyone is stressed. I dread to think how your bosses are coming down on you. I agree. Let's get this sorted. We start by tidying up the loose ends and listing out everything that needs to be done. Then we can delegate. Get half the team on the big projects, get the other half on clearing the small tasks, and then we can all bundle in at the end. Have you got an overtime budget, just in case?"

Amazing answer.

You started by validating your boss and connecting with them, normalizing how they feel by saying that anybody would understandably feel stressed in their position. You made your boss feel understood. Because you identified that your boss is looking for answers, you jumped straight into providing an actionable answer concisely and ended with a question, allowing them to give their input and progress the conversation forward productively.

What's more, you used your emotional intelligence to not minimize your boss's stress or anxiety, didn't take their comments personally, and didn't let emotion dictate your response. You could so easily have gotten angry or defensive with your boss coming to you but instead chose to stay neutral and diplomatic.

See the idea? Let's try another one.

You're having dinner with your partner, and the dreaded "Hey, can we talk about something?" comes up. I'll give you a rundown of the conversation, see what you would change and improve, and then we can go through it together. We'll use Mark and Sarah as an example.

Mark: "Hey, can we talk about something?"

Sarah: "Sure, what's up?"

Mark: "I've been thinking about how intimate we are, or in my eyes, how much we lack it. I want to be closer with you."

Sarah: "You want more sex?"

Mark: "Yeah. A bit more often, at least. I feel really disconnected from you."

Sarah: "I just don't want to. I get so stressed at work, and I'm so tired when I get home. I just don't have it in me. We've spoken about this before."

Mark: "Yup. I know."

Sarah: "So you're going to start sulking with me again?"

Mark: "Nope. You said you don't want to. I hear you."

Sarah: "No. I didn't mean that. I meant—"

Mark: "It's fine. It's whatever."

Sarah: "Can we talk about this?"

Mark: "Nope. You made yourself perfectly clear."

*Mark gets up and walks off.

Wow. Well, it feels like that conversation went well, yet it's almost certain we've all had a conversation like this, perhaps about a different subject, but along the same lines. There are so many issues with this conversation, and taking on board everything you've learned, you should be able to highlight the problems.

We'll go into a reformed example after this breakdown of the conversation.

Mark: "Hey, can we talk about something?"	A suitable introduction to a conversation. Not the best, but fairly casual.
Sarah: "Sure, what's up?"	Fine response, but since they were eating dinner, Sarah could put her knife and fork down, turn off any background music, show that she is preparing for the conversation, minimize all distractions, and give Mark her full attention.
Mark: "I've been thinking about how intimate we are, or in my eyes, how much we lack it. I want to be closer with you."	Not a very concise way of conveying his point, and it would perhaps be better if he had taken the time to think about his thoughts to present them more comprehensively.

Sarah: "You want more sex?"	No validation of Mark's feelings whatsoever. This is a very defensive response that Sarah is saying she can't be bothered to have the conversation. She just makes it seem like Mark is only interested in having sex, not addressing his point's emotional side. It's a very generic and hurtful response.
Mark: "Yeah. A bit more often, at least. I feel really disconnected from you."	Mark does well in not taking the blunt response personally and tries to portray the emotional side of how he feels, although his points could be made, again, more comprehensively.
Sarah: "I just don't want to. I get so stressed at work, and I'm so tired when I get home. I just don't have it in	Sarah, again, doesn't validate anything Mark says and instead gives a sharp reply that offers no productive progress. She then tries to cut the conversation short by saying this talk has already been spoken about before, basically saying that she

me. We've spoken about this before."	hasn't changed her point of view, doesn't want to revisit the subject, and won't change how she feels.
Mark: "Yup. I know."	Mark, feeling hurt by the conversation's bluntness, the lack of validation, and the unwillingness to communicate, shuts down and puts up his defensive barriers.
Sarah: "So you're going to start sulking with me again?"	Another hurtful comment. You can see where Sarah is coming from, especially if she is bored of the conversation and it has happened before, but there is zero empathy coming from her. Mark's feelings are only negatively validated.
Mark: "Nope. You said you don't want to. I hear you."	Mark is clearly done, and the conversation has fallen apart. Mark now resents Sarah for invalidating him and has disconnected completely. There

	are basically no chances at this point for the conversation to be redeemed.
Sarah: "No. I didn't mean that. I meant—"	Sarah notices the defensiveness, which triggers her own insecurities of her partner now pushing her away. She wants to be close with him and starts to try and pull him back into the conversation, now saying she'll listen.
Mark: "It's fine. It's whatever."	He's gone.
Sarah: "Can we talk about this?"	Sarah seeks validation and connection after being pushed away.
Mark: "Nope. You made yourself perfectly clear."	Still unresponsive.

Breaking this conversation down in such a way can show that so much of what we say and do has such a dramatic impact on the direction of which way the conversation will go. And this doesn't even take into account the body language that was going on!

Taking everything we've learned, let's go back to the beginning and try a much more productive way of having this conversation.

Mark: "Hey, Sarah. I've been thinking about something important to me. Are you okay to chat?"

Sarah: "Is it serious? Work was pretty intense today, but I can try my best."

Mark: "That's fine. We don't have to really go into it. It's more just something to think about."

Sarah: "Sure. Talk to me."

At this point, Sarah turns off the background music in the kitchen and puts down her knife and fork, giving Mark her full attention

Mark: "I was thinking about us and sex. I know we've spoken about this before, but I feel really disconnected from you lately, how with us both working so much. I feel like we lack intimacy."

Sarah: "Yeah. We don't spend as much time together as we used to. I feel disconnected from you as well. I just feel so tired all the time. I don't have the

156

energy to do anything for myself, let alone both together. But I do see where you're coming from."

Mark: "That's understandable. Maybe it's not about sex, but actually about doing something, well, anything together. Maybe bringing date nights back, or something like that?"

Sarah: "Yeah, I do miss our date nights. Remember when we tried to make a cake and forgot about it?"

Mark: "The oven still has burn marks!"

Sarah: "Well, how about this Friday, we get some ingredients and cook dinner together as we used to?"

Mark: "You focus on work. I'll grab some surprise ingredients when I'm done, so it's all ready when you get home, and we can get straight into it. Don't worry. It won't be a three-course meal. Just nice and fast so we can eat and cuddle. Want me to find a movie as well?"

Sarah: "That sounds perfect. Then, we can see what happens."

Mark: "It's a date."

See how different that conversation is? Both Mark and Sarah are acknowledging, empathizing, and validating each other and how they feel. They are both giving each other their full attention, staying calm and respectful to each other, and keeping the conversation moving forward productively.

Again, this doesn't even consider body language, apart from them both minimizing distractions, like eye contact and vulnerable posturing. Towards the end of the conversation, you can imagine them both laughing, making lots of eye contact at each other, and even winking in a flirty way, which is pulling them together.

To add to the conversation, if Mark or Sarah were unsure about how they were feeling, they would be able to ask each other questions for clarity. Instead, they did understand each other and were able to normalize how they felt (in this case, the feelings of disconnect or being tired due to overworking).

Apply this kind of logic in your own interactions. Whether you're at work, at home, with friends, or with family, taking what you've learned and applying it to your conversations isn't too difficult. Sure, it can feel like there's a lot to remember, but over time and by working on bettering yourself just one step at a time, you'll be amazed at how much of a difference it all makes.

Listening and having conversations in such a way can literally change your life.

Final Thoughts

Wow. What a journey that was, and what a conclusion. I'm hoping that now that you've read this book, you are already starting to apply these tips into your own life, and you're already seeing how much of a difference it can make. Remember, as with any self-improvement journey, your journey and results are unique to you, which is amazing since you get to be your own proof and see how quickly things can get better.

Being a good listener isn't just about hearing what people say. It's about being proactive in being an effective communicator that aims to make every relationship better and more fulfilling by using skills, experience, and knowledge in both human behaviors and psychology, all of which you now have a foundation of and will continue to expand on throughout your lifetime.

I would also like to take this moment to say that if you did enjoy this book, I would love to hear from you! You can reach out to me directly or simply leave a review on the platform where you purchased this book. It's always amazing to hear your thoughts and comments because writing books like this and sharing my experiences has been a passion for so many years now.

It's inspiring to hear your words of encouragement and how many benefits these books bring into your lives, and it's always good to hear what you think I can do better next time. I'm all about taking this journey and becoming the best writer I can be! Thank you for your comments in advance!

And that's about all from me! I hope you enjoyed reading this book and learned a lot. Hopefully, you're starting to see social interactions in a new and exciting way, and I wish you the very best on your development journey!

Also by James W. Williams

How to Read People Like a Book: A Guide to Speed-Reading People, Understand Body Language and Emotions, Decode Intentions, and Connect Effortlessly

Communication Skills Training: How to Talk to Anyone, Connect Effortlessly, Develop Charisma, and Become a People Person

How to Make People Laugh: Develop Confidence and Charisma, Master Improv Comedy, and Be More Witty with Anyone, Anytime, Anywhere

Digital Minimalism in Everyday Life: Overcome Technology Addiction, Declutter Your Mind, and Reclaim Your Freedom

Self-discipline Mastery: Develop Navy Seal Mental Toughness, Unbreakable Grit, Spartan Mindset, Build Good Habits, and Increase Your Productivity

How to Make People Like You: 19 Science-Based Methods to Increase Your Charisma, Spark Attraction, Win Friends, and Connect Effortlessly

How to Make People Do What You Want: Methods of Subtle Psychology to Read People, Persuade, and Influence Human Behavior

How to Talk to Anyone About Anything: Improve Your Social Skills, Master Small Talk, Connect Effortlessly, and Make Real Friends

References

Shrayber, M. (2017, March 8). *A Therapist Explains How To *Really* Listen To Another Human Being.* UPROXX. https://uproxx.com/life/how-to-listen/

Mednick, S. (2021, February 12). *The Power of Listening: Combating the 'listening deficit' in 5 steps.* Management 3.0. https://management30.com/blog/power-of-listening/

Weinstein, B. (2010, June 15). *Why listening is so difficult ... and what to do about it.* Reliable Plant. https://www.reliableplant.com/Read/25082/Why-listening-is-so-difficult

Why listening is difficult. (n.d.). Retrieved March 26, 2021, from https://saylordotorg.github.io/text_stand-up-speak-out-the-practice-and-ethics-of-public-speaking/s07-03-why-listening-is-difficult.html

Turner, A., Author: Ash Turner https://www.bankmycell.com/ Ash Turner is the CEO of BankMyCell. Following university graduation in 2003, Author:, & Ash Turner is the CEO of BankMyCell. Following university graduation in 2003. (2021, March 01). How many people have smartphones worldwide (Mar 2021). Retrieved March 26, 2021, from https://www.bankmycell.com/blog/how-many-phones-are-in-the-world

Lake, R. (2016, June 11). 23 attention grabbing attention Span statistics. Retrieved March 26, 2021, from https://www.creditdonkey.com/23-attention-span-statistics.html

Raab, D. (2017, August 09). Deep listening in personal relationships. Retrieved March 26, 2021, from https://www.psychologytoday.com/us/blog/the-empowerment-diary/201708/deep-listening-in-personal-relationships

Brendan McGuigan Last Modified Date: January 30, & Brendan McGuigan Date: January 30. (n.d.). What is selective hearing? Retrieved March 26, 2021, from https://www.infobloom.com/what-is-selective-hearing.htm

Many types of listening. (n.d.). Retrieved March 26, 2021, from http://changingminds.org/techniques/listening/all_types_listening.htm

Jacksonville, F. (n.d.). Fundamentals of public speaking. Retrieved March 26, 2021, from https://courses.lumenlearning.com/atd-fscj-publicspeaking/chapter/types-of-listening/

Notess, S. (2019, July 18). Listening to people: Using social psychology to spotlight an overlooked virtue: Philosophy. Retrieved March 26, 2021, from https://www.cambridge.org/core/journals/philosophy/article/abs/listening-to-people-using-social-psychology-to-spotlight-an-overlooked-virtue/BA713A91A6AAB3677336B1CC665C042B

Thieda, K. (2013, July 10). Easing partner PAIN: Six levels of validation. Retrieved March 26, 2021, from https://www.psychologytoday.com/us/blog/partnering-in-mental-health/201307/easing-partner-pain-six-levels-validation

Subscribe. (2016, September 26). The secret to being present in a conversation. Retrieved March 26, 2021, from https://www.watkinspublishing.com/the-secret-to-being-present-in-a-conversation/

6 tips for being present in every conversation. (2016, January 11). Retrieved March 26, 2021, from https://gentwenty.com/tips-for-being-present-in-every-conversation/

California, Y. (2020, October 15). Six ways you can validate a teen (and anyone else!). Retrieved March 26, 2021, from https://evolvetreatment.com/blog/six-ways-validate-teens-referents/

Shelley   Levitt
https://www.success.com/author/shelley-levitt/.   (-
0001, November 30). Go with your gut: The science of
instinct.   Retrieved   March   26,   2021,   from
https://www.success.com/go-with-your-gut-the-
science-of-instinct/

Communication - what percentage is body language?
(n.d.).   Retrieved   March   26,   2021,   from
http://www.bodylanguageexpert.co.uk/communication
-what-percentage-body-language.html

MasterClass. (2021, March 25). How to read body
language: 10 ways to recognize nonverbal cues - 2021.
Retrieved   March   26,   2021,   from
https://www.masterclass.com/articles/how-to-read-
body-language#5-ways-to-read-positive-body-language

Clukey, K., & Clukey, P. (2020, October 03). Confused
about what intense eye contact means? -get answers -
men & women. Retrieved March 26, 2021, from
https://confidencereboot.com/confused-about-what-
intense-eye-contact-means/

Gaille, B. (2017, May 23). 25 nose Growing statistics on
lying.   Retrieved   March   26,   2021,   from
https://brandongaille.com/24-nose-growing-statistics-
on-lying/

TEDtalksDirector. (2010, April 30). Lies, damned lies and Statistics (about Tedtalks). Retrieved March 26, 2021, from https://www.youtube.com/watch?v=1Totz8aa2Gg

Why people LIE – what Motivates Lying?: The psychology of lies. Retrieved March 26, 2021, from https://www.blifaloo.com/lying-why/

Statistic Brain. (2019, November 11). Lying statistics. Retrieved March 26, 2021, from https://www.statisticbrain.com/lying-statistics/

Sterling, D. (2017, May 24). The number one Reason relationships fail. Retrieved March 26, 2021, from https://www.psychologytoday.com/us/blog/ask-dr-darcy/201705/the-number-one-reason-relationships-fail

Domet, S., Jha, A., Hickman, S., Willard, C., Blakeslee, H., Staff, M., . . . Gerszberg, C. (2020, December 22). How to be more present, and stay present. Retrieved March 26, 2021, from https://www.mindful.org/how-to-be-more-present-and-stay-present/

MasterClass. (2021, March 25). How to develop your emotional intelligence - 2021. Retrieved March 26, 2021, from https://www.masterclass.com/articles/how-to-develop-your-emotional-intelligence#4-traits-of-emotional-intelligence

A cultural history of gaslighting. (n.d.). Retrieved March 26, 2021, from https://www.bbc.com/culture/article/20191122-cultural-history-of-gaslighting-in-film

www.ingramcontent.com/pod-product-compliance
Lightning Source LLC
Chambersburg PA
CBHW070755300326
41914CB00053B/660